THE IONIAN ISLANDS
TO RHODES

A SEA-GUIDE

Sea-Guides by H. M. Denham

THE AEGEAN
THE ADRIATIC
THE IONIAN ISLANDS TO RHODES
SOUTHERN TURKEY, THE LEVANT AND CYPRUS
THE TYRRHENIAN SEA

THE
IONIAN ISLANDS
TO RHODES

A Sea-Guide

H. M. DENHAM

W · W · NORTON & COMPANY · INC·
New York

First American Edition 1976

ISBN 0 393 03195 0

1 2 3 4 5 6 7 8 9 0

Contents

Illustrations

Maps in text by Aydua Scott Elliot and Elizabeth Scott

Line drawings by Madge Denham

Foreword

My earlier Sea-Guide, *The Eastern Mediterranean*, which covered a wide area, no longer provides enough detail to satisfy the increasing number of yachtsmen who now come to Greece and the Levant. They require considerably more information about the Ionian Islands and the mainland coasts of Greece and the Peloponnesus. New and up-to-date facts have been gathered during recent cruises, and the southern shores of Crete and Rhodes (with its dependencies) have also been more fully investigated. New anchorages have been chosen, not only for their own particular attraction, but in many cases because of their proximity to some interesting historical site.

Fellow yachtsmen have kindly contributed information about a number of ports and anchorages together with their facilities, and I am much indebted to them.

In order to keep the book up to date with the continual changes in physical features, the Royal Cruising Club has kindly agreed to co-operate by issuing the necessary amendments and additions in *Foreign Port Information*, (F.P.I.), which is available, not only to its members, but to those clubs affiliated which are eligible to receive copies of *F.P.I.* I am, therefore, very grateful to the Royal Cruising Club for this help. I want also to express my gratitude to Jehane West, who has doggedly pursued her Greek contacts on maritime affairs, and to Jane Boulenger, who once more has given me good counsel and help in guiding my book through many complications towards its final publication.

H.M.D.

Introduction

From the heel of Italy (Sta Maria di Leuca), the Otranto Strait is 70 miles across to the outlying islands of Corfu—the most northerly possessions of Greece. These delightful places, together with the Ionian Islands and the adjacent mainland coast, are the subject of the first chapter: not only do these shores offer a warm welcome to the cruising yacht but they deserve a prolonged visit, as much for their mountains and sheltered, indented coast as for the range of their historical interest.

On reaching Cephalonia, a decision must be made whether to turn eastward and approach the Aegean via the mountainous gulfs of Patras and Corinth or to continue southwards, following the open west coast of the Peloponnesus to Cape Malea. Before reaching Cape Malea another decision must be made: whether to enter the Aegean or to continue, passing southward of Crete. (See Chapter 3.)

The coast of southern Crete, seldom visited by yachts, is described in some detail, but although the scenery is wild and grand, these shores are not recommended to those in search of either safe shelter or the more sophisticated shore life.

Beyond Crete lies the eastern gateway to the Aegean, and, though inclined to be rather windswept, it is of interest to those who enjoy out-of-the-way places and primitive shelter. In this area is Rhodes, the one exception; here is both an excellent yacht harbour and every convenience of shore life.

Thus, as far as the comforts and fleshpots are concerned, after leaving the Ionian Islands and the entrance to the Gulf of Patras, one finds few amenities before reaching Rhodes, a distance of 400 miles.

GENERAL INFORMATION

Spelling of Place Names

Greek. During recent centuries, names used for islands and ports have very often been those given by the Venetians, e.g. the island of Kerkira was called Corfu; Zacynthos, Zante, etc. Some of these Italian names on the British charts are not now recognizable to the Greeks. If, for example, you enquire of a Greek for the harbour called St Nikolo in Kithera, he will not understand; the Greeks know this port only as Avlemona. Similarly, Cape Matapan to the Greeks is always Tenaron, Navarino is Pylos. All new British charts have now conformed to the Greek Hydrographer's names; but one must constantly be on the alert for changes in the new chart numbers.

Throughout this book I have observed the following system:

Such well-known places as Corfu, Crete, Rhodes, etc., I have written according to our English custom, but to make sure that every place may be easily found in the index, I have in most cases inserted the alternative name. For less well-known places I have used the spelling of the modern Greek name.

Port Officials are usually to be found at each port in Greece; even in a small port there is normally both a Customs Office and a Port Authority. In very small places the local policeman sometimes acts on their behalf. The harbour officials dress like the Navy, although they are not sailors, nor are they administered by the Admiralty. On a yacht's arrival a 'sailor' from this office will usually direct the yacht to a berth, and he will then ask for Ship's Papers. The complication of having both Customs and Port Authority papers has been overcome by the issue of what might be termed a 'Ship's Passport' (called a 'Transit Log' by the Greek authorities). This is issued at the Port of Entry on the yacht's arrival from her last foreign port.

A yacht must officially enter or leave Greece at one of the following Ports of Entry:

(a) West Coast: Corfu, Preveza, Argostoli (Cephalonia), Patras, Itea, Zante, Katakolon, Pylos (Navarino), Kalamata.
(b) The Aegean: There are a dozen ports including the yacht harbours at Piraeus.
(c) In the South: at Crete (on the north coast only) are the ports of Hania, Iraklion and St Nikolaos, and the main harbour at Rhodes.

Once a Transit Log is issued, it serves as a passport at each port of call in Greece; it contains detailed instructions. Its benefit to a yachtsman is that it usually enables him to buy duty-free fuel and also expedites formalities with harbour authorities.

Harbour Dues. These are not imposed on a yacht in Greece, unless it is at one of the new marinas.

Fuel and Water being important concerns for a small cruising yacht, the Greek authorities have now issued a list of 'Supply Ports' where these commodities can be obtained. At many places fuel and water have always been available, but now they are mostly supplied by pump and hydrant respectively at quays marked by blue and yellow zebra stripes. At major ports diesel fuel may be obtained without tax. Petrol must be bought from a local filling-station or store, in one's own containers.

It is not always advisable to fill the drinking-water tanks of a yacht from the hydrant or tap on the quay. Local people sometimes have good reason for buying their water from a spring in the country and, although more expensive to hire a water-cart, it is to the advantage of a yacht to do so too. As far as possible observations are made on the quality of the fresh water at the places listed.

Yacht's Mails. When visiting Greece it is normally quite safe to have one's mails directed c/o The Harbour Master at any significant port that the yacht may be visiting.

In other countries of the eastern Mediterranean it is sometimes advisable to ask the British Consul to help.

Food and Drink. As the enjoyment of cruising in the eastern Mediterranean can be so easily marred by stomach troubles, a few notes on the local food and drink are necessary.

Very few English digestions are immune to eastern Mediterranean cooking, which is often very greasy with strong olive oil added to almost everything. In all the small restaurants in Greece it is quite in order for the customer to enter the kitchen and choose his dish from the wide copper pans spread out on the charcoal stove—generally there are chicken, lamb stew, stuffed tomatoes, savoury rice, and fish soup, etc., all looking most inviting, as well as the Greek dishes such as *dolmades* (meat and rice in vine leaves); *moussaka* (a sort of shepherds' pie with cheese on top), and *pasticche* (baked macaroni with meat and cheese). These should be avoided in the evening as they were probably cooked for the mid-day meal and have been re-heated. Usually there is a charcoal grill, and lamb cutlets or fish cooked on this is a safe bet; but be sure to say 'without oil' (*ohee ladhi*) when ordering or you will find cold olive oil has been poured over your grill. Fish is almost invariably good and fresh. Nearly all restaurants have little dishes of yoghourt, and also delicious *baklava* (honey cakes with almonds). Never order your whole meal at one time, or you will find that the dishes will be brought all together, and by the time you have eaten your first course the second will be congealed.

In early spring the following are usually available:

Fish

Tsipoúra	French Dorade
Sinagrida	Sea Bream
Barbounia	Mullet
Maríthes	Whitebait
Octopóthi	Octopus
Calamári	Squid
Astakós	Lobster
Garídes	Prawns

Meat

Arnáki	Lamb ⎱—often good
Hirinó	Pork ⎰
Brizóles	Chops
Bon Filet	Steak (fillet)
Móskari	Veal
Nefró	Kidneys—usually good

Butter used to be obtainable only in Athens, Corfu and other towns much frequented by tourists, but today the situation has been much improved.

Fruit and Vegetables. Early in the season there are oranges, cherries, loquats, beans, peas and courgettes.

Some of these begin to go out of season in May and are followed by tomatoes, cucumbers, aubergines, lettuces, peaches, apricots and figs. Later there are grapes and melons.

Anything eaten raw should be washed with a few grains of permanganate of potash.

Wines

Kampá or *Plaka*, both red and white in bottles, is obtainable at ports near Athens.

Etálya, a dry white wine, is quite pleasant and can be bought on draught.

Deméstica, a dry white, can be bought in bottles at many places.

Retsína can be bought everywhere except in Crete and the Ionian islands.

Local vermouth and brandy are passable aperitifs: *Ouzo* (a form of *Raki*) is the local spirit and is obtainable everywhere on draught.

'Fix' beer and similar brands are obtainable nearly everywhere, and are excellent.

Bottled soft drinks either with water or as concentrate are exceptionally good.

Health. The incidence of typhoid and tetanus varies from year to year in certain places described in this book, but there is always some, and it is sensible to be inoculated.

Practically all the well-known medicines and drugs can be bought in Athens and possibly in the few big towns mentioned, but nowhere else, so it is advisable to have a well-stocked medicine chest. The *Yachting World* diary gives an excellent and comprehensive list which covers most eventualities. Two useful additions are sulphathalidine and enterovioform, as, inoculated or not, many people in the Mediterranean, particularly if eating ashore, become afflicted with what is vaguely known as 'stomach trouble'.

Nowadays in Greece there is no trouble in finding a doctor on the larger islands, and even in the smaller places there is generally a qualified medical practitioner, a chemist, and, at the worst, probably a midwife. *Sailing Directions* mention the hospitals to be found at the larger ports; in most of the Ionian Islands the hospitals are modern and appear to be efficient.

As good health largely depends upon the purity of the drinking water, it is advisable to take the opportunity of filling a yacht's tanks where possible at the places recommended in this book.

Fishing. Off the shores of Greece a variety of fish (see previous page) is caught both by day and, when the moon is down, by night. An attractive sight at many a small port is the evening departure of the *grigia*, the mother-ship towing the net-boat and five 'ducklings'—each fitted with two large gas lamps. They usually remain on the fishing ground all night, not returning to harbour until the sun is well above the eastern horizon.

Tunny, which people now believe spawn in the central Mediterranean, are caught in that area in long and complicated nets, called *mandragens*, usually laid off prominent headlands in Sicily and Tunisia. Only small numbers of tunny visit the eastern waters, although in Greek and Roman days they were a constant source of food for the people.

Of the non-edible fish two very unattractive species are sometimes seen:

Mackerel-sharks up to 12 feet in length are sometimes met with offshore. Usually seen on a steady course, they seldom go close to the land, although every two or three years one hears of someone being attacked. Sting Ray, Torpedo or Electric Ray are very occasionally met when bathing off a shallow unfrequented beach. This is especially so in spring when the young are being hatched, and it is easy to step inadvertently on a ray half buried in sand. A sting may have serious consequences and should be dealt with at once and the poison extracted.

There are also flying-fish which from close-to are fascinating to watch. Although seldom airborne for more than about 15 seconds they have been estimated to fly at 35 knots and to make flights of 200 yards or more.

Dolphin is the great companion for a yacht in open waters. When sailing on a steady course a whole school may suddenly be seen approaching at high speed effortlessly rising and dipping through the waves. Having reached the yacht they will surround her and amuse themselves swimming backwards and forwards under the keel with a knowing upward look at the humans peering down at them from the upper deck. When tired of this game, another spurt and the shoal is gone, their course being marked by splashes receding into the distance.

There are two species of dolphin in the Mediterranean, the bottle-nose and the common dolphin; the latter can be recognized by the long, narrow beak and somewhat finer features, dark brown back and white belly with stripes of grey, yellow and white on either side; when full grown they can be 8 feet long, and are immensely powerful swimmers capable for a short while of making 30 knots, although a cruising speed of about 15 is preferred. Being mammals they must surface at intervals to take in air; this they do through a crescent-shaped hole in the head, like the blow-hole of a whale. The beak is purely for catching the fish on which they live.

Lately there has been a revival in the cult of the dolphin, and they are recognized as having a high degree of intelligence, many stories being told of their becoming tame. In antiquity some of the great writers, including Aristotle and Pliny, made their observations on the dolphin, which was always regarded as the friend of man. Herodotus tells of the young poet Arion of Lesbos, who, when returning from Sicily, was threatened by mutinous sailors intent to rob and murder him. Fortunately Arion was a player of the cithera, and the music of this instrument had attracted a passing dolphin to the ship; when

Dolphins in Minoan days. Frescoes on the walls of Knossos. There appear to be fewer dolphins in Greek waters today than there were a few years ago.

Arion jumped into the sea to escape his would-be murderers he was rescued by the dolphin which eventually set him down safely on the shore.

The easiest way to join or leave a yacht in Greece is to choose a port with air connection via Athens. These are: Corfu, Igoumenitsa (bus connection with Ioanina), Aktion (for Preveza), Kalamata, Hania (Khanea), Iraklion (Heraklion) and Rhodes. Some routes have only one daily service, others two or three, according to the season and the popularity of the place.

Two airports were opened in the Ionian Islands in June, 1971: one at Zante, the other at Argostoli, each with a daily service to Athens.

There are also frequent steamer connections from Piraeus with most of the major ports, but the schedules are continually changing according to the season. On the mainland one can also travel to and from most places by bus; the roads have recently been much improved.

PILOTAGE

Charts. The most valuable information both on pilotage and archaeological matters is to be gleaned from the older charts made by Her Majesty's surveying vessels and from observations by travellers in the early part of the last century.

On modern charts some of the smaller plans of minor ports are no longer printed, because this information is now considered to be redundant. Nevertheless, if you happen to possess the old charts it can be seen how valuable and accurate they are, and how little changed these coasts would be but for the following:

(1) **Removal of Ruins.** Looking back on the last few years it is surprising how much the man-made features have changed in Greece since the early British surveys were made. At that time most of the ancient sites were much more extensive than they are today, especially in the more remote places, where buildings and masonry have largely vanished—in a few places completely: thus certain landmarks are no more.

(2) **Changes in the sea-bed.** In some areas, usually those susceptible to earthquakes, the sea-bed also has changed in character and depth; occasionally a conspicuous above-water rock has toppled over, or a pot-hole has appeared where one might have anchored.

When details of sea-marks, depths, lights, etc., require some elucidation, or are at variance with information furnished in official publications, I have endeavoured to remark on them in this book.

The Hydrographer of the Royal Hellenic Navy has recently had surveyed a number of small ports and anchorages of interest to yachts. These charts, now published by the British Hydrographer, may be bought from Admiralty Chart agents; but they no longer show the hatching to indicate mountains and torrent beds, which can be so helpful to a yacht when in pilotage waters.

Important. Admiralty Mediterranean Pilot Books should always be consulted.

Prevailing Winds and Weather.

Between Corfu and the mainland the winds are mostly N. to N.W.; at night light land breezes spring up from East.

West Coast of Greece: mostly northerly, occasionally off the land, light to moderate.
Kithera Channels: westerly, fresh to strong at times.
Southern Crete: northerly squalls from the high mountains.
After abnormal spring rainfall a thick haze often lies over the mainland, and the Ionian Islands during the summer, when visibility may be reduced to 4 or 5 miles or less.

Weather Forecasts in English, French and German are transmitted on the Greek National Programme (412 metres) at about 0740 and again after the News at about 1940 daily.

xvi

Currents. In the summer months there is no appreciable current by the Ionian Islands, but in the Kithera channels a west-going stream up to 1 knot may be expected. The current off southern Crete is negligible and between Crete and Rhodes south-going.

Laying-up Ports and Repairs. Yachts normally stay afloat during the winter-months and may be moored by arrangement with the local Greek authority at one of the Piraeus ports, Porto Cheli, or at Rhodes, etc. A few yachts can be hauled out, the best facilities being provided at one of the Perama yards near Piraeus.

At the Piraeus ports (Passalimani and Vouliagmeni) refitting and slipping facilities are close at hand at the Perama yacht-yards and arrangements may also be made for receiving yacht stores from England without paying duty. These ports, therefore, are the first choice.

Running Repairs. During a cruise it may be necessary to make good some misfortune which is beyond the scope of ship's resources. It is then a matter of chance whether or not outside help can be obtained. At many islands and small ports in Greece there is a boatbuilder, or a joiner's shop or a mechanic in the village willing to help; sometimes quite unexpectedly one comes across a caique sailor who has experience in making sail repairs.

Although the Greek National Tourist Organization now issues a chart denoting certain ports where repairs to a yacht can be undertaken, one should realize that very few places here or elsewhere in the eastern Mediterranean have had previous experience with high-grade yacht work.

Berthing. In Greek ports yachts normally berth with an anchor laid out to seaward and stern to the quay. Some form of gang-plank is desirable.

This method of securing has certain advantages: the yacht's side does not get rubbed by the quay; one has some privacy from the gaze of onlookers; but, perhaps more important still, one is less likely to be invaded by cockroaches or other vermin which sometimes frequent the quayside. In this unfortunate eventuality, the only successful way to eliminate the pest is to purchase Fumite tablets (obtainable through Boots the Chemist), and having sealed all apertures, ignite the tablets as directed and leave the yacht for 24 hours.

Local Craft in Greek Waters
The lugsail rig—'standing and balance lug'—was, until very recent years, to

be seen everywhere in Greece. Up to the period of the First World War square topsails were also hoisted on the fore. Motors had not then been introduced.

Nowadays, very few small Trehandires with the lugsail rig are to be seen off the Ionian Islands. Most of them carry only steadying sails.

THE IONIAN ISLANDS AND THE
MAINLAND COAST

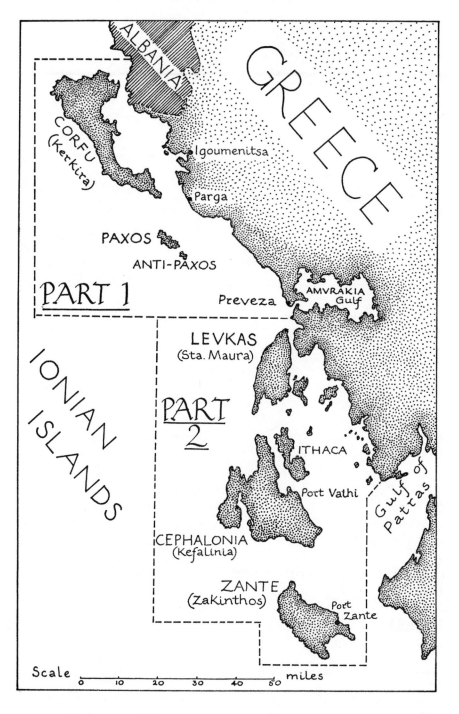

ALBANIA

GREECE

CORFU
(Kerkira)

Igoumenitsa

Parga

PAXOS

ANTI-PAXOS

PART 1

PREVEZA

AMVRAKIA
Gulf

LEVKAS
(Sta. Maura)

IONIAN

ISLANDS

PART
2

ITHACA

Port Vathi

CEPHALONIA
(Kefalinia)

Gulf of
Patras

ZANTE
(Zakinthos)

Port
Zante

Scale _____ miles

0   10   20   30   40   50

PART I

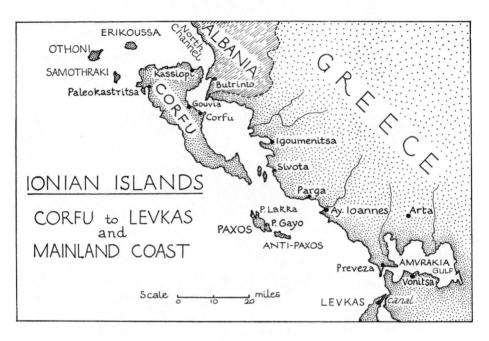

I

The Ionian Islands
and the Mainland Coast

PART I: *CORFU, TO LEVKAS, AND THE ADJACENT COAST*

The Island of Corfu

Spread like a shield upon the dark blue sea.
The Odyssey v.281

Since Hellenic days, when its traders set out to found colonies on the Mediterranean shores, Corfu has almost continuously played its part in maritime history: Thucydides* refers to 'that splendid armament which was destined to perish at Syracuse'; 400 years later Caesar's ships passed en route to Actium, and here again after another twelve centuries Don John of Austria led his fleet from Corfu to annihilate the Turks at Lepanto.

Later Corfu, together with the other six Ionian Islands, was for some centuries under the sovereignty of Venice whose influence is still in evidence in the names and features of some of the inhabitants as well as in much of the architecture. When Venice fell in 1797 these islands passed to France, then, after changing hands a number of times, to Britain under a Protectorate which she maintained until 1864, when they reverted to Greece.

During the First World War the Serbian army was evacuated here, and a memorial to those who died was erected on Vido Island, which is sometimes visited by Yugoslav warships. In 1920 the town was bombarded by an Italian warship, and in the last war the island was occupied by the Italians and Germans.

With a population of 36,000, Corfu town, capital of the Ionian Islands, is largely Venetian in architecture with some French houses on the seafront and

---

* *Victory song was sung, the pouring of libations brought to an end, and the fleet moved in column out of harbour. Once open water was reached . . . they pressed on with all speed for Corcyra.* History of the Peloponnesian War (XVIII).

English Georgian public buildings by the Palace Square. Another legacy of the English is the game of cricket, and on the occasion of a visit by one of H.M. ships the local club usually turns out an eleven. Ginger-beer can also be bought.

The country, with its many villages, is beautiful with luxuriantly wooded mountains and everywhere green with colourful shrubs and wild flowers. The large unpruned olive trees, gnarled and very old, are a legacy of the Venetians; their oil is still good today.

Climate. The summer temperature reaches well into the nineties, yet the climate is not oppressive. In the spring the place is known for its humidity and in winter for its heavy rainfall. 'There is no winter' wrote Edward Lear, who made many visits to the Ionian Islands, writing and painting with much enthusiasm.

Winds on the eastern side of Corfu seldom conform with the official forecast for the Ionian Sea. During the summer nights and well into the forenoon there is invariably a gentle easterly land breeze followed by a calm; but towards noon a light N. to N.W. 'day breeze' predominates, occasionally coming in from N.E. Sometimes this light breeze may be whipped up into a fresh Maestrale. Only on about one day in four can a S.E. breeze be expected.

A weather forecast in French, German, Greek and English is transmitted daily on the Greek National programme (see p. xviii)

Approaching the Island. A yacht may be fortunate in approaching Corfu in the early light when few sights can be more beautiful than the distant Pindus mountain range described by Byron in *Childe Harold*:

> *Morn dawns; and with it stern Albania's hills,*
> *Dark Suli's rocks, and Pindus' inland peak,*
> *Robed half in mist, bedew'd with snowy rills.*

Chart 206 shows the Corfu Strait, the northern passage of which was closed to navigation for twelve years after the mining of H.M. Destroyers *Saumarez* and *Volage* on 22nd October, 1946. Since no diplomatic relations exist between Britain and Albania, the shores of this country should be avoided by yachts— even in daylight. When approaching from westward by night Albania's mountain villages, lit by a blaze of electricity, may be seen a great distance off.

Near the narrowest part of this strait—a mile across—may be seen a few small houses of the Albania outpost at Butrinto. The Venetians maintained it as a port until Napoleon's time, its defences having given it the title of 'The Key to Corfu'. Nothing of the defences now remains; only a customs house and some fishermen's cottages can be seen; but a couple of miles inland are the excavations of a small Greco–Roman town. The river, which flows from a large lake, enters the sea at Butrinto after passing over a shallow bar. The whole area was famous for an abundance of game and, until the Second World War, was visited annually by British shooting parties.

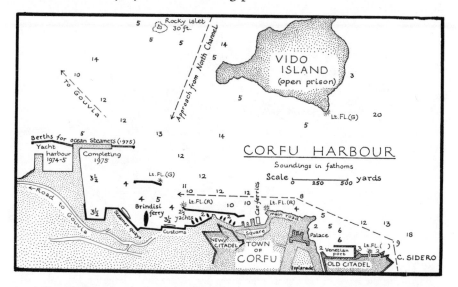

For convenience the above sketch-plan shows Vido Island and rocky islet about 500 yards closer to Corfu than they actually are.

The Port

Berth. See Chart 725. The Venetian galley port under the 'Old Fort' is now reserved by the Navy, and yachts should therefore make for the Commercial port where berths are allocated at the yacht station eastward of the steamer quays. This is not always an agreeable place to lie, especially in strong N.W. winds when it can be dangerous. It is, however, possible for some yachts to berth inside the detached mole, but the depths of nearly 2 fathoms cannot be depended upon, and the place can be smelly. Caiques are continually moving in and out.

In the event of bad weather from the N. and N.W. it is advisable to move to Gouvia, or alternatively to proceed round Cape Sidero into Garitsa Bay and anchor south of the citadel. (*See pp. 7 and 8.*)

Officials. A Port of Entry—Harbour, Customs, Immigration and Health. There is a naval commandant and a British Vice-Consul.

Facilities. Fuel and water at the yacht station. A number of restaurants and tavernas, provision shops, banks and modest hotels are within 10 minutes' walk. Ice from a factory also 10 minutes' walk, but delivery can be arranged. Electrical and engineering repairs can be arranged by the boatman. A 5-ton crane is available at the Customs Quay. The more fashionable part of the town is by the Palace Square and the better modern hotels are outside the town.

Communications. Daily ferry service with Brindisi, Igoumenitsa and Patras (for Athens)—frequent car-ferry to Igoumenitsa; coastal steamers and cruise ships call regularly. Air connections with Athens and Italy, also twice weekly with London.

The Town

Following the coastal road towards the town one comes to the large English palace of St Michael and St George. Built of sandstone brought from Malta in 1816, part of this building is now used as a museum for Greek and Roman finds, and also a collection of Ming. The Palace looks out upon the spacious esplanade which, being raised high above the sea, provides beautiful views across the massive citadel known as the 'Old Fort' towards the mountains of Epirus on the mainland coast opposite. The sides of this large square are flanked by a long facade of eighteenth-century three-storey French architecture whose tall arcades not only form an appropriate background for naval and military ceremonial parades, but also blend themselves most propitiously into the gay cafe-restaurant life where Corfiots come to foregather here in the cool of the summer evenings. The present-day Corfiots have sprung from families much intermarried with Venetians during the earlier centuries of Italian influence. There is also in Corfu town a small Jewish community, much reduced after the German exterminations in the Second World War.

Shore Excursions

A number of places on the island are easily accessible by taxi or bus. Apart from Paleokastritsa on the N.W. coast and a number of bathing beaches on the north coast, there are some interesting places to be seen just south of the town:

Kanoni or 'One Gun Battery' (its former English name) overlooks the spacious lagoon of Khalikiopula, the former harbour of the Corcyran–Athenian fleet more than 2,000 years ago. At that time it was deeper and more extensive, for it is only recently that the airport has reclaimed much of its inland area. From the Tourist Pavilion at Kanoni one can enjoy the well-advertised view across the two islets guarding the entrance to this shallow but picturesque lagoon.

Anchorage. The southernmost of the two islets, Pondikonisi or Mouse Island, has 2-fathom depths close northward where a yacht may anchor temporarily in pleasant surroundings. This, however, is no longer a peaceful anchorage, as it lies exactly in line with the airport runway.

On the hillside of the tall peninsula which divides this lagoon from the sea lies the site of the early Greek fortified capital at Analypsos. This stronghold continued until medieval days when the Venetians came to build the new city and the New Fort. Most of the stonework of the ancient city was then used as a quarry. Towards the sea lies *Mon Repos*, which is the country residence of the Greek royal family, was originally built some decades ago as a country-house for a British governor. It was here that Prince Philip was born in 1921. The estate runs down towards the sea where there is a pier. Above this is a spring of fresh water which was used by the wooden ships of the Royal Navy early in the last century.

The *Achilleion*, now a casino, was built originally as a summer palace for the Empress Elizabeth of Austria, and was used for some years later by Kaiser Wilhelm II for his spring holidays. The vaunting inscription set up by the Achilles' statue 'To the greatest of the Greeks from the greatest of the Germans' has now been removed.

Emergency Anchorages in event of strong North to N.W. winds at Corfu Harbour:

Gouvia (Chart 725), an all-round sheltered bay, three miles N.W. of Corfu is useful when strong N.W. winds make the port untenable.

There are usually no buoys or stakes to mark the approach channel which affords depths of more than 20 feet. A stone pier now extends from near the Venetian galley sheds off the extremity of which there is anchorage for large to medium-sized yachts in 3 to 4 fathoms with good holding in mud. Cloudy water. A more sheltered anchorage suitable for small yachts is to be found in the northern part of the bay in 2½ fathoms.

Approach directions for entering Gouvia *See map.* From Gouvinon Island, steer about N.N.W. for the islet off Cape Kommeno. When reaching position (a) 200 yards from the islet, turn westwards and head into the inlet towards a conspicuous villa on the point. When 200 yards off the point in position (b) turn about 40° to port and head for conspicuous galley shed lying close N.W. of a stone pier, at the same time keeping about 150 yards offshore until

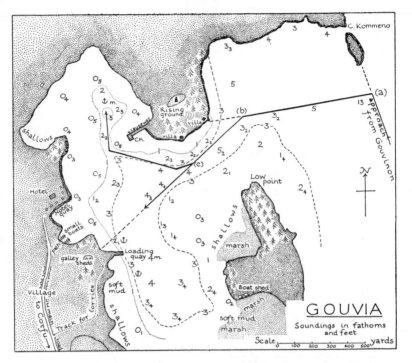

The data on the above plan is largely taken from a recent Greek survey but certain landmarks and amended soundings have been added.

reaching position (c), i.e. when the second conspicuous villa is abeam. **A medium-sized yacht** proceeding to the deep-water anchorage should then continue on the same course until reaching the vicinity of the pier. The **small yacht** wishing to enter the more sheltered northern anchorage should continue on her course, as shown in plan, maintaining a distance of 150 yards offshore until nearing the conspicuous white chapel standing on the extremity of a causeway. Here, proceed with caution aiming to pass 120 yards off the chapel—sound carefully and turn northwards towards the anchorage.

Getting ashore by dinghy at either of these anchorages is difficult on account of the soft mud. Apart from the hotel quay, it is recommended to try the small boat basin. There are shops and restaurants in Gouvia village, but the drinking water is obtained from wells. A half-hourly bus service reaches Corfu town in 15 minutes.

Garitsa Bay, on the south side of Cape Sidero, provides useful shelter in strong northerly winds if the yacht harbour should become untenable.

The anchorage is close southward of the old British garrison church of St George, to be recognized by its handsome Doric facade. There are depths of 4 fathoms on mud; good shelter from North and West. The above-water rocks can be seen. A small boat and swimming harbour was being constructed close by. In event of the wind shifting to S.E. a yacht can move over to the shelter of the small local yacht harbour at Anemoilos which was dredged in 1970.

OTHER ANCHORAGES

In Corfu Bay

Dassia, an open bay by the Club Mediterranee close northward of Gouvia, is pleasant as a temporary anchorage if one anchors in the southern corner. In calm weather a yacht may anchor close off the beach where there are small hotels, restaurants and tavernas.

Kalami, Agni and **Kouloura** (the latter recognized by the white Venetian mansion) are attractive coves all shown on Chart 726. Kalami is the best choice; anchor in 4 fathoms at the head of the bay. The bottom is thin weed on sand. A small *pension*, once the house of Laurence Durrell, can provide a meal. Kouloura, the most attractive, is impractical as a secure anchorage.

Sta Stefano (Kariotiko), close to the narrow strait, has good anchorage at the foot of the naval observation post. It is part of a military area and one should inform the Naval Commandant if intending to come here.

Outside Corfu Bay

Kassiopi (Imerolia), lying on the north coast about 2 miles west of North Channel, is incorrectly shown on the new Greek Survey (Chart 726).

A short mole protects a very small harbour where it is possible for a medium-sized yacht to berth only in settled weather.

Berth. Secure head or stern to the mole and lay out a kedge. The bottom is largely weed and boulders.
Facilities. There are some shops and a couple of tavernas.

The ruined fortress on the headland was built by the Angevins of Naples in the fourteenth century. The Venetians, later in possession of Corfu, fearing its capture by the Genoese, destroyed it. Kassiopi was formerly a Homeric site and later a Roman settlement. It was here that the emperor Nero 'danced and sang' during his travels in Greece.

Alipa and Ayios Spiridion (Chart 26) on the west coast are suitable anchorages in settled weather, but entirely open to South. Alipa is the better and more spacious anchorage—3 fathoms on a sandy bottom. A supply buoy is moored off. Ashore is a government pavilion, restaurant, and bars. The place is now over-run by tourists on account of nearby Paleokastritsa. The monastery should be visited, and those with sufficient energy should ascend the steep track leading to the castle of St Angelo, high above.

The Outlying Islands of Othoni (Fanö) and Erikoussa (Merlera)

Both these islands are partially cultivated and wooded with small hamlets inland. The anchorages are on the south coast and can be identified by a few small houses on the water-front.

Othoni is tall (1,300 feet) and green on the south side and is the more interesting of the two.

Approach should be made with caution in order to clear the rocky shoals (less than 6 feet) which lie 3 cables south of the anchorage. Coming from the East a yacht should pass southward of the shoals and turn towards the land when the eastern edge of the cliffs bears East of North. The shore may then be followed at a distance of half a cable until reaching the anchorage. Coming from the West there is no difficulty; the S.W. point of the Island is lit and there is deep water half a cable offshore.

Anchorage in the bay is in 4 fathoms, anywhere convenient on clear sand, excellent shelter except with winds from southerly quadrant which are rare in summer. In emergency, however, one might have to shelter on the north side of this island; although it is possible to get an anchor down where a 4-fathom mark is shown on the chart, this can only be found with great care; a bed of clear sand with 4- to 5-fathom depths can be located 200 yards offshore, north of a cleft on the hillside. Here there is good shelter both from the southerly winds and sea.

The small boat harbour on the S.E. corner of the island, which is rockbound, has depths of only 3 to 4 feet and is used only by some local caiques.

Erikoussa lies relatively low compared with Othoni; it has a very small population, and attracts a few summer visitors.

Approach. At both headlands of the bay underwater rocks extend further than the chart implies.

Anchorage. Rocks protrude above the sandy bottom on the west side of the bay near some bollards. The N.E. corner is better and the water is very clear. There is no suitable anchorage on the north side of this island.

At both these islands police are the only officials. As regards facilities, Othoni has a small bar and a summer tavern. Bread, eggs, fish and sometimes crawfish can be bought. Erikoussa cannot offer so much. At both islands the water is from wells.

Both these islands are renowned for their crawfish, many being sent to Corfu by local caique, which maintains daily communication (6 hours) with Corfu.

About 1,500 people live in Othoni and barely 1,000 in Erikoussa but the populations are dwindling as the young men leave to seek a livelihood elsewhere. In summer one or two yachts call with under-water fishermen, and others when on passage to or from Italy.

There is no particular history attached to these islands, but, during the British occupation of the Ionian Islands a subaltern's detachment was stationed at Fanö which was then popular in spring for the quail shooting.

> *Go in thy glory o'er the ancient sea*
> *Take with thee gentle winds*
> *thy sails to swell.*
> JOHN WEBSTER, Yacht *Wanderer*, 1850

Proceeding southward from the port of Corfu one reaches the **Island of Paxos (Paxoi),** one of the smallest islands of the group, 5 miles long, of oval shape and partly wooded; but, aside from its olives, it produces very little because it lacks water. Of the two harbours, Port Gayo is the more charming; but if time permits, Port Lakka, in the north of the island, is well worth a visit en route.

Port Gayo. A minute, but most attractive harbour with complete shelter beside a charming little hamlet. Suitable for small- to medium-sized yachts.

Approach. See plan on Chart 723. Yachts drawing more than 6 feet must use the northern entrance. The southern entrance, though lit, is used only by local craft. If approaching from the mainland coast care should be taken to avoid the Madonna Shoal, lying in position 2¼ miles east of Madonna Lighthouse. Here the Venetians once lost a treasure-ship and in 1817 two British frigates struck.

Berth. Opposite the village square off the projecting quay, or on either side of it with the anchor laid out eastward. There are depths of over 2 fathoms. Beware of the yacht station where the depths are only 3 feet.

Facilities. One or two provision shops and some modest tavernas. Daily ferry to Corfu, bus to Lakka. A summer hotel lies about one mile southward along the coast.

The little houses and church form a charming setting to the square. The only tall house was once the British Residency, and here Gladstone spent a night in 1858 when visiting the Ionian Islands. A road leading from the village to the top of the hill provides a pleasant walk with views over the island. One may also land on the islet, among the ruins of the fortress.

Longos, consisting of a few houses tucked into the corner of an open bay, looks attractive from seaward, but it is actually of little interest.

> **Approach.** Chart 206. Care should be taken to avoid the Paxos Reef, lying about 4 cables offshore. There are also some rocks close to the point on the southern shore.
>
> **Anchorage** is on a sandy bottom in 2 fathoms, or a small yacht may berth close inside a short mole (10 feet) affording some shelter from east.
>
> **Facilities.** A couple of shops and tavernas. A bus service between Gayo and Lakka calls near here.

Port Lakka. A broad but shallow bay with a small hamlet, lying in attractive surroundings with good shelter.

> **Approach.** Chart 206. *Sailing Directions* gives a good description of the entry. There is no difficulty by day. The depths on the sand bar have a minimum of 11 feet, and there is slightly more water to seaward of the quay.
>
> **Anchorage.** There is 3 fathoms off the quay, where the bottom is clear sand. In a N.E. wind there is a swell, though the shelter inside the harbour is good in all weather.
>
> **Facilities.** The hamlet is primitive, although a small supply of fresh provisions is obtainable. In 1971 there were two tavernas and a cafe. Fresh water from the village pump. The Corfu ferry calls daily and berths stern to the quay. A bus runs to Gayo.

On the S.E. corner of the island is the deserted inlet of **Spuzzo Bay.** Its unspoilt surroundings are attractive, and a yacht can choose where to anchor according to the wind. Off a large ruined house there are convenient depths and good shelter. A track leads to Gayo.

The Island of Anti-Paxos is small with only a few score of inhabitants; it is of no particular interest. The anchorage is in the bay on its eastern side where fishing craft sometimes haul up. Supplies are obtained from Paxos when weather permits. The island grows some vines from which a small quantity of unpalatable sparkling red wine is produced.

On the east coast are some wonderful bathing beaches so far untouched by tourism.

THE ADJACENT MAINLAND COAST

On the chart may be seen a number of bays along this mountainous coast, some are well sheltered according to the direction of the wind and make an interesting anchorage for a yacht.

Under summer conditions a land breeze springs up at dawn, lasting for 3 or 4 hours, followed by a calm. The N.W. breeze begins to be felt towards noon.

Corfu: coastal view from Paleokastritsa

The medieval bridge at Arta

Parga: view towards the citadel

Following the shore southwards from the Albanian frontier, richly wooded mountains rise steeply above the coast, and opposite Corfu there are a number of anchorages, few of which are used, as yachts usually prefer the attractions of Corfu:

Ftelia, tucked into the mountains; has a choice of two deserted creeks suitable for an anchorage.

Pagania. A completely landlocked bay, said to be poor holding.
   Note. The above harbours lie in a military area and in 1970 were forbidden to yachts.

Igoumenitsa (Chart 723). A small port under the Pindus range lined by a sandy shore off a plain of olive groves. The place has become important as a terminal for the Italy–Greece motor-car ferry service. A Port of Entry.

Approach. Chart 206. This broad bay has a narrow channel marked by three pairs of buoys near the outflow of the river. Here the current occasionally flows swiftly.
Berth. A broad quay, for mooring the car-ferry and other steamers, has sufficient space for a yacht to berth on the shoreward side where it is well sheltered, but there is sometimes a great demand for berthing space.
Facilities. In the village fresh provisions and fuel may be bought; there are three or four small hotels and restaurants. A daily bus service reaches Athens in 15 hours. The large car-ferry takes 10 hours to Brindisi, and there is also another car-ferry to Corfu running several times daily.

13

The port lies in a pleasant setting, but has no particular interest other than the scenery. One can drive by taxi or bus to Ioanina (Janina), an ancient town on the lush shores of an elevated lake. There is bus connection with Preveza; also a short excursion to be made to the ancient site of Dodoni.

Twenty miles south of Corfu and on the eastern side of the southern approach are two uninhabited wooded islands:

Islets of **Sivota** and **Ayios Nikolaos,** and the adjoining cove of **Mourzo.** The surroundings are attractive, but apart from the scenery there is no other interest, and there are only limited possibilities of anchoring.

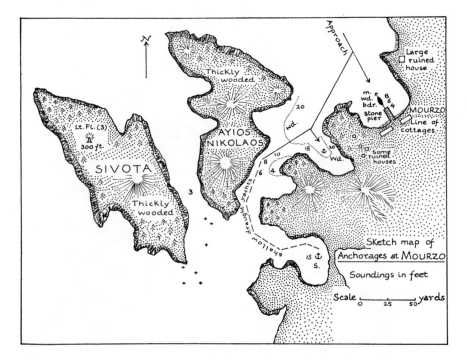

The approach should be made only from the north, for the southern entrance is encumbered with rocks. This place is suitable only for small to medium-sized yachts.

Mourzo, although stated to be a yacht station, has only a shallow jetty (4-feet depth at its extremity). The sea-bed is heavy weed and boulders and the cove is exposed to the day breeze. Some very poor little houses line the shore, where one can sometimes buy bread or fruit.

The channel between the two islands affords a depth of only 3 to 4 feet, and that between Ayios Nikolaos and the mainland 6 feet. Small yachts of about 5-feet draught have passed through and anchored in a small cove behind an islet. The only other suitable places to anchor are shown on the sketch plan, although occasionally a yacht anchors between the islands north of the shallow passage where it is exposed to the day breeze.

Known as the Swine Islands in antiquity, these two islands supported a mainland village where Mourtos now stands—the 'continental Sivota' of Thucydides, where the Corinthians once erected a memorial no longer to be seen, to commemorate a sea battle.

Only 100 years ago travellers reported the presence of deer and wild boar; and at the beginning of this century these islands and the other places on the coast already referred to, were well known to shooting parties from the large yachts that came here in early spring and October; the abundance of game—quail, snipe, woodcock, partridge and duck—continued to attract shooting parties until recent years.

The steep mountainous coast trends to the S.E. for 12 miles until reaching Parga.

On Suli's rock and Parga's shore,
Exists the remnant of a line,
Such as the Doric mothers bore.
BYRON, *Don Juan*

Parga. A delightful village standing on the slopes overlooking two pleasantly sheltered bays.

Approach. Plan on Chart 723. The prominent objects mentioned in *Sailing Directions* are easy to discern. A bright light is exhibited at night.

Anchorage. Though a few yachts prefer the more eastern of the two bays on account of easy access to the town, it is more comfortable during normal fine weather conditions to anchor in the sandy western bay. By anchoring near the extremity of the ancient mole one avoids the discomfort of the swell caused by the day breeze.

In 1971 the small ancient harbour was dredged to 12 feet in the middle, but the ballasting of the restored mole protrudes about 20 feet under water. Thus only one or two small yachts can take advantage of this improved shelter.

The eastern bay is quite tenable in the early forenoon before the breeze springs up. A pile pier projects for 30 yards from the centre of the bay; at its extremity are depths of almost 2 fathoms. If requiring fuel or water it is recommended to lay out an anchor to seaward and haul in the stern to the pier-head.

Officials. Harbour Master and Customs.

Facilities. Near the water-front are shops well stocked with fresh provisions. There are restaurants, tavernas and two modern hotels. Fuel and water at the pierhead. Ice can be bought. Bus communication with Levkas and Igoumenitsa.

The ruined Venetian castle dominates the village whose inhabitants, together with those of two neighbouring hamlets, number about 2,000. They are mainly engaged in the cultivation of olives. The village with its winding streets, old white houses and stairways is charming and quite unspoilt. A summer camp for tourists has been built on the slope near the convent on the high ground of the western bay. East of Parga is an open bay where in 1971 hotels were growing up.

Ayios Ioannes—Chart 723 (plan)—lies in a beautiful mountainous setting, and is suitable as a summer yacht anchorage, provided the wind keeps north of west. Anchor on the west side in Skuluki Cove. The bottom (mud) shelves steeply and a warp ashore may be necessary.

There are no habitations, but a road with bus communication passes above leading to Parga.

Port Fanari, or **Phanari,** a bay, open to winds between S. and W., and apart from a discomforting swell after the day breeze, it is sheltered from other quarters. It lies by a flood plain formed by two rivers; its position can sometimes be located at a distance by the ruins of a castle on the mountains $2\frac{1}{2}$ miles eastward of the entrance.

> **Anchorage.** Chart 723. Proceed towards the north corner, according to draught, and although there is much less water than charted, there is sufficient depth for small vessels to swing to an anchor.

There is a good beach for bathing in the S.E. corner of the bay near the mouth of the River Acheron, but the water is colder than normal and is discoloured by the river water. A number of fishermen's houses have recently sprung up round the shore.

Proceeding S.E. one follows the green mountainous shores, often well-cultivated and with occasional beaches, until reaching

Cape Kastrosikia, 12 miles southward which provides an indifferent anchorage in 3 fathoms. Sheltered by some reefs from the west winds, it is, however, very rock-bound, and is used only by a few small fishing craft which, during bad weather, haul out on the beach.

Remember the moment when Preveza fell
The shrieks of the conquer'd, the conquerors' yell;
BYRON, *Childe Harold*

Preveza. An unattractive little commercial port with interesting associations.

Approach. (Chart 1609) which is interesting, and there should be no difficulty until nearing the end of the dredged channel when the tidal stream sets at about 40 degrees to the ship's course.

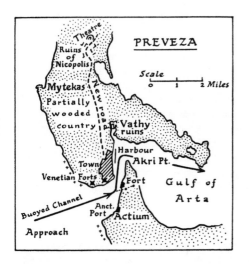

The channel, alleged to be dredged to 24 feet, is in places only 16 feet and never more than 20 feet.

Berth. The safest place is at the northern end of the quay just inside the low harbour mole. Here the tide is slight and the depth 2½ fathoms; one can haul in stern to quay —only caiques berth at this part. There is also a recently constructed inner basin which provides complete shelter.

It is pleasant to anchor in wooded surroundings at the head of the bay which used to lead into **Vathy**; unfortunately a causeway now closes the former basin. There is good shelter and holding with enough room for a medium-sized yacht to swing.

Officials. A Port of Entry. Customs and Port Authority and Immigration.

Facilities. There is a water hydrant at the southern end of the quay, and though the water is unharmful, it is chalky. Market and provision shops are of good standard. There are three mediocre hotels, a new bank, and several tavernas. One can usually buy good fish which is caught in abundance inside the gulf. The meat, too, is usually good. Gas cylinders of all types can be filled while you wait at a gas factory on the road to Nicopolis about 1½ miles out of town and beside Port Vathy.

The quays along the water-front have recently been improved and the town of twelve thousand people has now acquired a modern look after many years of Turkish influence.

The hinterland is flat and extensively planted with olives. Much of the fish from the Gulf of Amvrakia is brought to Preveza and then carried by lorry to Patras and Athens.

Three miles to the northward are the extensive ruins of Nicopolis, built by Octavian (later styled Caesar Augustus) to commemorate his victory in 31 B.C. when he defeated Antony in the Battle of Actium.

17

History. The battle was the outcome of the Civil War which following the assassination of Julius Caesar in 44 B.C. had been resumed. The two contestants were Octavian controlling the western part of the empire and Antony the east. Each had large armies which together with the rival fleets finally came within striking distance of one another in the early spring of 31 B.C.

Octavian's fleet, mainly Liburnian galleys, had based themselves at Mytikos (where the blocks of the harbour mole can still be seen) and Antony's fleet, largely triremes, used the well-sheltered anchorages at the entrance to the Gulf of Amvrakia close to Actium. Here the rival fleets supported by their encamped armies remained most of the summer months, Antony's men being far from content with this passive role.

According to Plutarch, Antony felt by the end of August that his chances of victory were waning and when he finally decided to put to sea he realized that morale was low. He first burnt his unmanned warships, embarked his treasury in merchant vessels, put aboard the triremes' sails—an unusual practice before battle—and embarked a large number of soldiers. One morning early in September the fleet put to sea in a flat calm and soon sighted the galleys of Octavian lying in wait at the mouth of the estuary. The two fleets remained in sight quite inactive until about midday when the prevailing wind began to set in freshly from north-west. Now Octavian's galleys plunged in to attack the less numerous triremes of Antony which they soon began to overpower.

In mid-afternoon during the heat of the action a vessel was seen to hoist a purple sail and passing through the fighting was soon heading to pass north of Levkas. This was Cleopatra bound for Egypt closely followed by Antony (as Shakespeare wrote 'like a doting mallard') abandoning his men to continue the losing battle. They soon fared even worse due to the weather, for according to Plutarch, many triremes were sunk by heavy seas in the late afternoon.

A year later Antony and Cleopatra had committed suicide, and Octavian had restored the Roman Empire and celebrated his victory by building Nicopolis. Nicopolis grew to become a fine city, being enriched during Justinian's reign with large public buildings. It continued as a centre of Christianity into Byzantine times, and flourished until the end of the ninth century when, after invasion by Slavonic tribes from Bulgaria, its destruction was completed by a severe earthquake. The theatre, city walls and a couple of churches still stand, and even though the city has largely subsided beneath the waters of the gulf a visit to the ruins is still worth while.

Sixteen centuries later the strategic position of Preveza was realized by Turkey's great pirate-admiral Barbarossa. After conquering the Aegean Islands and then Crete in 1538 he turned his attention to the Venetian possessions of the Ionian Islands, then protected by a modern fleet of galleons and galleys under the command of Andrea Doria. His base was Corfu, and when his escorts passed down the coast, protecting Venetian merchant ships trading to Zante, Ithaca, Santa Maura, etc., the Turkish galleys at Preveza would pounce upon them whenever they chose. This they did with such crippling effect that the Venetian forces were withdrawn and Barbarossa soon earned himself the title 'King of the Sea'. It was not until some thirty years later, long after Barbarossa was dead, that the Christian fleet finally defeated the Turks at the Battle of Lepanto. (*See page 4*)

The Gulf of Amvrakia (Arta) extends for nearly 20 miles inland, and although it has a number of anchorages on both sides it is of limited interest to the

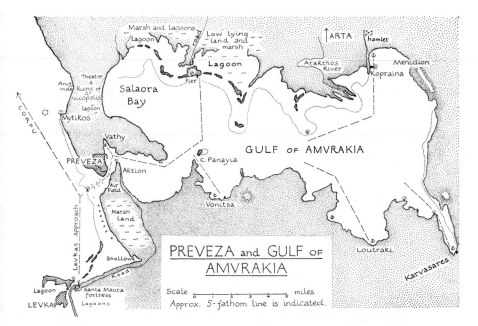

PREVEZA and GULF OF AMVRAKIA

Scale — miles
Approx. 5-fathom line is indicated.

average yacht. The northern shores, especially, are low and swampy, and until recent years malaria was prevalent. Almost more alarming is the warning in *Sailing Directions* that 'these marshes are infested by snakes and reptiles, some of which are venomous'. Despite these objections, English shooting parties coming here early in the century used to make their headquarters at Salaora, and came away with plentiful bags of woodcock, snipe and duck.

Vonitsa, lying on the southern shore, is a dull village in a pleasant setting beneath a large Venetian fort; it has a reasonably sheltered anchorage with quays off the village.

> **Anchorage.** Chart 1609 shows the anchorage. The short pier with a lighthouse (Lt.Fl.R.) has depths of 10 feet at its extremity. Although a few boulders extend under water the end of the pier can be useful for hauling in a small yacht's stern. Alternatively anchor one cable off. The day breeze normally stirs up only a short sea of no consequence at the anchorage.
> **Officials.** Harbour Master and Customs.
> **Facilities.** Meagre supplies of fresh fruit, etc. at the shops. One or two poor tavernas. A fresh-water tap 30 yards from the quay.

Vonitsa is dominated by an uninteresting, but extensive, Venetian castle and has behind it a cultivated plain. The completion of the new motor road may well improve its present low standard.

Aliki (Kopraina Bay) lying in the N.E. corner of the gulf is near the mouth of the Arakthos River which, having flowed from the ancient town of Arta, now enters the sea. Shallow-draft fishing craft use this river which is claimed to be navigable for 4 miles, and even as far as Arta. Arta, which is of historical importance is visited sometimes today on account of its medieval bridge and the Byzantine church, but the present village of 10,000 people has no attraction.

Both the Arakthos River and a smaller stream enter the gulf side by side and have built up extensive sandbanks to seaward where fishing craft are often busy and many species of wild birds can be seen. The area requires careful exploration.

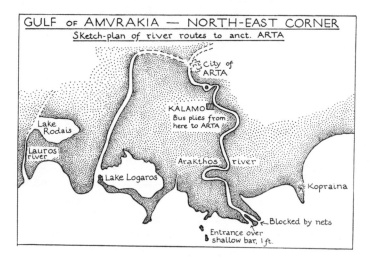

Directions

Enter Arakthos River by the southern entrance (1 foot on bar). The mouth of the northern stream is blocked by nets.

After the junction of the two river mouths the depths in mid-stream are about 3 to 6 feet as far as the islet above Kalamo.

At Kalamo village there is a good bus service to Arta.

Alternatively, it is claimed that a more attractive venture is to enter the River Lauros and proceed by this river to Arta.

Anchorage. The easternmost sandspit, which is now overgrown with bush, extends south-wards for a mile forming the western arm of Kopraina Bay. About 300 yards north of its extremity is a broad white tower (Lt.Fl.W.R.). When approaching, this should be kept fine on the port bow and the low-lying spit followed at a distance of a cable until arriving in the N.W. corner of the bay where there is anchorage in 5 fathoms, mud bottom, open to the south.

The place is flat and deserted; remains of an old harbour, quay and warehouses are the only shore objects; but there are a number of small fishing boats and a variety of wild birds. This corner of the gulf would be of interest only to those who enjoy exploring rivers by dinghy and bird-watching.

On the eastern shore of the bay is the modern little resort of Menidion skirted by the new motor road which runs round the head of the gulf.

Karvasares Bay, lying in the S.E. corner of the Gulf, has a loading quay, visited by small steamers, at the foot of Amfilokhia village. At the head of the bay is a narrow spit with 10-feet depths, off which a yacht may anchor. *Sailing Directions* gives warning that near the end of this spit, during the last century, a small volcano erupted on two occasions, killing most of the fish in the Gulf and covering the water with sulphur as far as Preveza.

Near Amfilokhia village are remains of an ancient city with two walls ascending from the beach towards the hill on which are foundations of numerous square projecting towers.

Loutraki is a bay with a primitive hamlet. One can anchor conveniently off a sandspit, but the place has no particular interest.

Salaora Bay is boarded by low sandy shores enclosing lagoons behind. Eastward of the light is a disused short stone pier with $2\frac{1}{2}$-fathom depths at its extremity; but other than a road there is nothing else.

PART II: THE ISLANDS OF LEVKAS, ITHACA, CEPHALONIA, ZANTE AND THE ADJACENT MAINLAND COAST AND OFFLYING ISLANDS

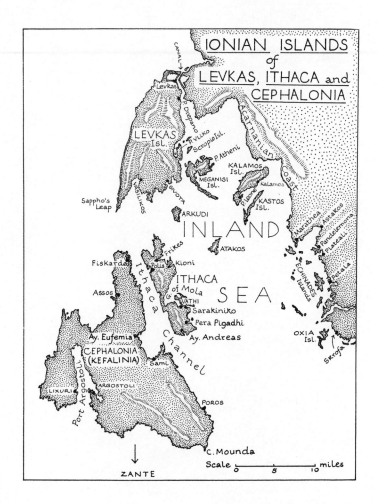

ISLAND OF LEVKAS
(SANTA MAURA)
  The Canal
  Port Levkas
  Port Drepano
  Port Vliko
  Sivota Bay
  Vasilikos Bay
  Sappho's Leap
ISLAND OF ITHACA (ITHÁKI)
  Port Vathi
  Frikes
  Kioni
  Sarakiniko
  Pera Pigadhi
  Ayias Andreas
  Pis Aeton
  Polis
ISLAND OF CEPHALONIA
(KEFALINIA)
  Port Argostoli
  Lixuri
  Port Assos
  Fiskardo Bay
  Ayias Eufemia
  Sami
  Poros

NEARBY SMALL ISLANDS
  Moudra Islet
  Meganisi Island
    Port Atheni
    Port Vathy
  Scropio Island
  Kalamos Island
    Port Kalamos
    Port Leone
  Kastos Island

ADJACENT MAINLAND COAST
  WITH OFFLYING ISLETS
  Marathea Bay ⎱ Dragamesti Bay
  Astakos ⎰
  Pandelemona
  Plateali (Platea)
  Kamaros Bay
  Petala
  Skrofa
  Dragonera Islets
  Echinades Islets
  Oxia Island

ISLAND OF ZANTE (ZAKINTHOS)
  Port Zante
  Port Kieri
  Port Vromi

PART II: *THE ISLANDS OF LEVKAS, ITHACA CEPHALONIA, ZANTE AND THE ADJACENT MAINLAND COAST AND OFFLYING ISLANDS*

The Island of Levkas

The Santa Maura of the Venetians, Levkas is only an island by virtue of the canal cut through the swamps which separate it from the Acarnanian coast. It is mountainous with a central ridge rising to 3,700 feet running from N.E. to S.W. The north and west coasts are bare and uninviting, but opposite the mainland the valleys open out towards the shore, the country is green and there are attractive villages with orange and olive groves. Although the main port has little attraction there are some delightful wooded inlets on the S.E. of the island as well as the circular, and almost enclosed, bay of Port Vliko. Edward Lear paid a number of visits to the island where he painted many attractive landscapes. The extensive oak forests to be seen inland in his day have largely disappeared, and so have the deer. In the villages many of the women still wear traditional dress and devote much time to beautiful weaving.

The greatest menace to Levkas is the earthquakes, one occurring every twenty to thirty years. The last severe upheaval was in 1948 when Cephalonia and Ithaca were also damaged. Another, but less severe, earthquake followed five years later.

The Canal
Approach. Chart 1609 shows the canal approaches which can be negotiated easily by day and, with care, by night.

(*a*) *If coming from the north* one can see the Venetian fortress of Santa Maura standing out over the flat country some miles off, and as one draws appreciably closer the structure on the extremity of the northern entrance spit becomes clear. However, when a yacht is sailing towards this dead lee-shore—perhaps for the first time—one may become anxious at the delay in sighting the actual entrance, especially when being driven along by a Force 6 afternoon breeze. You may see the fortress of Santa Maura, but because the land all appears as one the extremity of the northern spit cannot easily be discerned. It will eventually show itself in transit with Santa Maura light tower on a bearing of 193°.

Coming from Paxos, a south-easterly course leads one to Fort Tekkes, easily distinguished from a few miles distant. When about a mile from the canal entrance you can then turn on the transit bearing 193°, and head for the entrance.

On entering, the extremity of the northern spit should be given a berth of 50 yards, and one should then turn into the canal leaving two can buoys to port. The small cable ferry which plies frequently, shows 'not under control' shapes when operating.

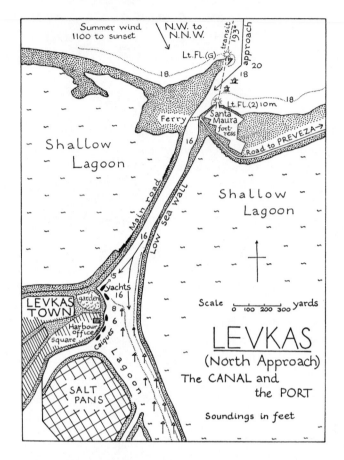

Summer wind 1100 to sunset

N.W. to N.N.W.

transit 193°

approach

Lt.Fl.(G)

20

18

18

Lt.Fl.(2)10m

Ferry

Santa Maura fort-ress

Road to PREVEZA→

Shallow Lagoon

16

Main road

Low sea wall

Shallow Lagoon

16

yachts

16

garden

LEVKAS TOWN

8

6

Harbour office

Square

Caiques

Lagoon

SALT PANS

Scale

0 100 200 300 yards

LEVKAS

(North Approach)

The CANAL and

the PORT

Soundings in feet

(b) **If coming from the south** the large fort of St George makes a distant landmark. Three pairs of buoys mark the entrance, and there are well-placed perches marking the channel all the way to the port.

The canal is used by small steamers and caiques and is claimed to have a minimum depth of 17 feet. A pilot is not compulsory.

The canal and the long northern breakwater were built by the Anglo–Ionian Government in the middle of the last century. There had, however, been canals before; the early Corinthians dug one which subsequently silted, only to be re-dug by the Romans which in turn must have filled in during the Middle Ages.

The Port is merely a well-sheltered quay at the elbow of the canal, beside a growing village recovering from the 1948 earthquake.

Berth. A yacht requiring fuel or water should berth as indicated in the plan, i.e. off the Yacht Station in 14-feet depths. The bottom is mud, good holding, and there is good shelter. The place is cooled by a seldom failing sea-breeze. There is considerable traffic at this quay, both yachts and caiques. If wishing to stay for more than a few hours, a yacht would probably be requested to berth alongside the quay.

Officials. Harbour Master and Customs.

Facilities. Apart from fuel and water, there are plenty of provision shops. Ice can be bought at a small factory, 10 minutes' walk. Restaurants and tavernas are nearby, and a small modern hotel has been built by the main square. Levkas produces a very good light Retsina wine.

The village of 8,000 people has slowly recovered from devastation of the last earthquake, and its economy is now fully restored. The church of Pantocrator, built by Morosini to commemorate the Venetian conquest of 1684, follows the classical Venetian style. There are three other churches built later, including the small St Demetrius with some holy paintings in oils. A small museum (with icons from damaged churches) and the library are close to the main square.

Port Drepano, at the southern entrance to the canal is no longer a port. The protecting mole lies submerged and unmarked, as shown on Chart 1609, i.e. it runs almost east and west between the projecting point of land and the port-hand entrance buoy—west of Volios Island; its eastern extremity is about 20 yards S.W. of the buoy. The chart shows two temporary anchorages: a shallow one north of the mole and a deeper one south of it. Both are good holding, but exposed completely to the southern quadrant, a direction to be feared only in event of thunderstorms or passing depressions. A primitive hamlet lines the shore, and a new short mole, one cable southwards, affords shelter to caiques which are frequent callers. Salt is shipped away from extensive salt pans on the lagoons.

There is no purpose in anchoring at Drepano, and most yachts coming southward call at either Meganisi Island (see page 28) or at Port Vliko. The green wooded shores should be followed, where a new motor road has now been built to link Port Vliko with Port Levkas.

Before entering Port Vliko one passes the very small wooded **Islet of Moudra.** On its western side immediately above the water's edge, a handsome baroque house stands out boldly against the pine trees. For many years it has belonged to the Valaoritis family, who have frequently played a prominent part among the intelligentsia of Greece (see photograph, facing p. 45).

Port Vliko (see photograph, facing page 29). An entirely enclosed spacious bay with a hamlet, lying at the foot of mountainous slopes. On the western side of the entrance is the market garden hamlet of Nyddri; on the opposite side immediately south of the entrance point is *an unnamed cove* with an attractive anchorage for three or four yachts in depths of 3 to 5 fathoms. The shore is green and partly wooded, and near here is the villa built by the distinguished German archaeologist, Dörpfeldt. Early in the century he made discoveries of Mycenaean remains in the countryside above Vassiliki after which he began to expound the theory that Levkas, and not Ithaca, was the original home of Ulysses. A small museum of archaeological finds is close by.

Inside Vliko Bay there is:

Anchorage as convenient either off the hamlet or off the small settlement on the opposite side.
Officials. A Harbour Master from Nyddri may call in his motor-boat to see the Transit Log.
Facilities. The best place to shop is Nyddri. There is difficulty in obtaining fresh water.

OTHER ISLANDS IN THIS AREA. See map, p. 23:

Meganisi Island, indented on the north side with two suitable inlets each forming a pleasant night anchorage for a yacht.

Port Atheni, a long, attractive, deserted inlet with almost all-round shelter.

Approach and Anchorage. Chart 3496. The entrance is well marked. Head up the more southern of the two arms and anchor near the head of the inlet in 4 to 5 fathoms.

A few fishing craft use a jetty at the head of the creek. Farming country all round and no dwellings in sight from the anchorage.

Port Vathy, close by, is similar to Atheni, but slightly less convenient for depth and shelter. The main hamlet lies at the head of the inlet.

A couple of miles to the N.W. lies **Scropio Island** owned by Mr Aristotle Onassis. Scropio, seen from seaward appears as a beautiful parkland estate, and in the bay on the west side of the island is often moored Mr Onassis' yacht. A road now encircles the island and one can see the small houses for the employees, generating plants and storehouses.

Note. About one cable east of Scropio is a dangerous rocky patch almost submerged. Also on Chart 1620 is shown the rocky shoal between Scropio and the north of Meganisi.

Kalamos Island is relatively large and tall with a farming population who mostly live in the hamlet beside the small harbour on the S.E. coast. A mole 150 yards long extends in a northerly direction, curving towards N.N.E. near

Levkas: Santa Maura fortress

Fishermen drying octopus in the shallow lagoons of Levkas

Levkas: looking southward showing the entrance to Port Vliko on the right

its extremity. It protects the harbour from normal summer winds, but it is entirely open to N.E.

Anchorage is in the middle of the harbour in depths of 3 fathoms. Sand and short weed. (The depths close off the mole are too shallow and irregular to permit a yacht to moor close off.)
Facilities. A fresh-water tap by the root of the mole, a taverna; bread and vegetables can be bought.

The island is seldom visited by a yacht.

Port Leone, though rather deep is sometimes more comfortable than the main port, especially in strong N. winds when gusts come off the mountain.

Kastos Island, narrow, tall and with occasional patches of cultivation, lies only half a mile S.E. of Kalamos. The small hamlet on the east coast stands above a cove which can be distinguished by a mill on the ridge above.

The uninhabited islands of Arkudi and Atakos are without an anchorage.

Returning to the south of Levkas is Sappho's Leap,

> *The very spot where Sappho sung*
> *Her swan-like music, ere she sprung*
> *(Still holding in that fearful leap,*
> *By her lov'd Lyre) into the deep.*
> THOMAS MOORE, *Evenings in Greece*

Sappho's Leap lies on the open sea. There is no anchorage here.

The broken white cliff on the S.W. corner of the island stands out and is clearly marked on the chart. From the top of this perpendicular cliff (200 feet above the sea) and sloping precipitously into the landward side is the 'ancient mount' beneath whose shadow Childe Harold 'saw the evening star above Leucadia's far projecting rock of woe'.

Apart from the well-known legend of Sappho, the leap was used, according to Strabo, for other purposes: on the Festival of Apollo it was the custom to cast down criminals from this headland into the sea, but to break their fall birds were attached to them. If a criminal reached the sea uninjured, boats used to recover him.

On the S.E. side of the island there is suitable anchorage at **Vasilikos Bay** (Chart 720), which is rather open, and has a small boat harbour off the village where the moles afford protection from the south.

Approach. The new plan is misleading. The first or outer mole is destroyed and largely under water; it could be dangerous at night. The second mole (with a light at its extremity) has 12-feet depths nearby, and off the quay on the north side where medium-sized yachts may berth with the prevailing breeze blowing freshly broadside on.

The day breeze, however, sweeps down from the hillside in strong gusts from the N.W. often making boatwork, from the anchored yacht, somewhat uncomfortable. The hamlet of small houses, built of timbered frames and either of stone or brick, typical of Levkas, has no particular interest. Water and fuel are available at the quay.

Sivota Bay lies at the head of a narrow, wooded inlet with natural all-round shelter and perfect solitude in most attractive surroundings. One or two farmsteads are near the shore and a hamlet approached by a rough road is a mile and a half inland.

The anchorage has good holding in 3 fathoms. A water-tap supplied by a running stream is on the western shore.

The Island of Ithaca (Itháki)

And when arose the brightest of all stars which heralds the dawn, the sea-wandering bark drew near the Island of Ithaca. There is a harbour there sacred to Phorcys, the Old Man of the Sea.

HOMER, *The Odyssey.*

Ithaca is an attractive island of historical interest and well worth visiting in a yacht.

Port Vathi. A delightful little port in a charming mountainous setting, capital of the island. (See illustration facing page 44.)

Approach (Chart 1620), is easy, day or night. A War Memorial has taken the place of the fort marked by the chart on Hill 254. A yacht must pass eastward of the islet with the small white church when approaching the port.
Berth. Either anchor off the steamer quay or berth temporarily stern-to, having in mind that mail steamers are apt to arrive without much notice. An alternative for a single small yacht is to berth alongside in the very small inner harbour which has 10-feet depths close to its outer mole.
Officials. Harbour Master and Customs, but there is no Immigration Officer.
Facilities. Water and fuel are not easy to obtain at the Town Quay; but at the exposed yacht station on application to Shell in the town, they can be laid on. There are modest restaurants and tavernas on the sea-front. Ice is obtainable and also provisions. Mail steamers on the Athens–Corfu run call frequently in summer.

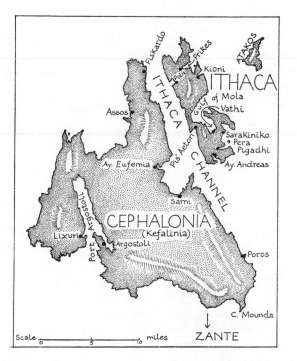

After the serious earthquake of 1953 the port and buildings along the sea-front were rebuilt, and trade has since gone ahead, especially the export of wine and olives.

A pleasant walk follows the quay along the western side of the bay. One comes to a small public garden with a plaque commemorating Byron's visit to the island in 1823. It is said that he used to row out to the islet with the chapel for his morning swim.

Although the association of Homer's *Ulysses* with this island has usually been accepted, Professor Dörpfeldt contends that during the Middle Ages, when these islands were evacuated by the inhabitants, they lost their original identity. The Ithaca of Homer he believes is really Levkas. There are, however, few people today who uphold his belief, but a number of excursions by motor-car to the alleged sites are made daily by tourists visiting Ithaca.

> *In Ithaca there are no wide courses, nor meadowland at all. It is a pasture land of goats, and more pleasant in my sight than one that pastureth horses, ...*
>
> HOMER, *The Odyssey.*

A steep road takes one up the slopes of Merovidi, (above the town), to

31

Perachora, the site of the old Greco-Roman settlement. From here is a magnificent view: beneath lie the fiords and Port Vathi, the Ithaca Strait can be seen reaching out to Sami (the home of Penelope's twenty-four suitors), and to the east are the 'summer isles of Eden lying in the dark purple spheres of sea'.

Towards the northern half of Ithaca, an hour's drive brings one to Stavros, the site of the Homeric capital. From the cluster of unsightly modern villas and small cafes now springing up on this dominant saddle the land slopes steeply down to the sea on either side: on the west to the deep circular bay of Port Polis (Chart 720) whence it is claimed the expedition sailed for Troy, and on the east to Port Frikes lying at the head of a small inlet.

Frikes, Chart 720. Though it is an attractive inlet it is often spoilt by the violent gusts which the day breeze shoots down the valley every afternoon. A short mole and one or two small houses at the head of the sandy steep-to inlet give the little port an appeal.

> **Approach.** A solitary windmill on Cape Akrotiri indicates the south side of the approach to the inlet.
> **Berth.** A short mole has 2-fathom depths near its extremity which is marked by a Lt. Fl.(R). Secure the stern to the quay and lay out an anchor with as much cable as possible, the holding being uncertain. The afternoon breeze and sometimes a swell makes the little port uncomfortable, especially the strong gusts of wind.
> **Facilities.** There is not much to be obtained in the port, but a rough road leads up to Stavros about one mile up the valley.
>
> The port is used for the export of agricultural produce grown on the fertile plain on the north of the island.

Kioni. A delightful sheltered bay with a small village and summer villas tucked under the hillside.

> **Approach.** Chart 720. The three old windmills on the slope south of the entrance are easily distinguished.
> **Anchorage.** Let go off the village quay, at the head of the bay where shelter is good but holding uncertain. Some yachts prefer to run a warp ashore to a sea wall in the N.E. corner. Anchorage off the cemetery has usually been found to be satisfactory.
> **Facilities.** A few shops and tavernas are near the water-front. A caique ferry plies from here to Port Vathi during the summer months.

On the S.E. side of the island:

Sarakiniko Cove is most attractive. It affords reasonable shelter, good holding and is entirely deserted.

> **Anchorage.** Chart 203 provides sufficient detail. A yacht could anchor at the head of the bay

as convenient; a large yacht needs to anchor in 6 fathoms and run out a warp to an olive tree by the shore. The bay is open only to the S.E., normally a safe direction in summer.

One may land at the head of the bay, and climbing up a steep bank enjoy a delightful view across to Port Vathi which can be approached by a track; it is little more than a mile distant.

Pera Pigadhi, near the S.E. tip of the islet is shown on Chart 720. A pleasant open summer anchorage in calm weather.

Anchor in 5 fathoms on a sandy bottom (occasional rock) whichever end of the channel that shelter might be needed. Suitable for small yachts.

There is no sign of habitation and nothing of interest ashore.

Ayias Andreas—a deserted mountainous bay in picturesque surroundings.

Anchorage. Chart 720. Let go in 5 to 7 fathoms off the shingle beach, but there is very little room to swing and the holding is uncertain.

There is no habitation or means of communication with the interior.

It was here that Telemachus is believed to have landed on his return from Sparta to avoid capture by the suitors of Penelope. The stables of Eumaeus were on the hills above; rising beyond a white cliff is a glen with a recess in the rock filled by a never-failing spring. Here, according to tradition, is Homer's Fountain of Arethusa, where the swine of Eumaeus were watered.

Inside the Ithaca channel on this island's west coast are two anchorages: Chart 720 shows those of Polis and Pis Aeton.

Polis is a broad and deep open bay facing S.W. A yacht may anchor at its head where the bottom rises steeply to 5 fathoms.

Facilities. There is nothing close at hand, but one may land in the dinghy at a small boat camber and walk to Stavros (30 minutes) on the saddle of the hill. Limited fresh supplies.

Many believe that close by Polis stood the Homeric capital of the island.

Pis Aeton is an open, deserted bay with only a ruined house near to which a yacht can find convenient depth to anchor. The bottom being hard sand, the holding is uncertain, and also the bottom has been reported recently as being fouled by an electric cable.

The Island of Cephalonia (Kefalinia)

This is the largest and most mountainous of the seven islands, and disposed over the four main villages has a population of about 60,000. Both Homer and

Strabo refer to it as rugged and mountainous; it certainly lacks the soft beauty of Corfu. The lofty ridge which crosses the island from N.W. to S.E. rises to a largely bare summit called the Black Mountain (5,380 feet); it is easy to identify at a great distance to seaward. Pinewoods cover some of the lower slopes; on the foothills are the vineyards which grow the currants for export, and there are some cornfields; but the island generally lacks water.

The main port is Argostoli, and, although a Port of Entry, it is not the most convenient one for a sailing yacht on account of the tall mountains surrounding it.

Port Argostoli. The sheltered arm of a large natural harbour by the main village (7,000 inhabitants) of the island. (Chart 1557.)

> **Berth.** Either lay out an anchor and berth stern to quay or secure alongside southward of the new quay which affords good shelter, even in N. winds. This part of the quay is inside the harbour gate, and therefore fairly private.
>
> Alternatively, one may anchor off according to draught, but this is somewhat exposed to the afternoon breeze which may reach Force 5 or even 6 in late summer.
>
> **Officials.** Police, Health and Harbour Officials. A Port of Entry where an unusual charge on foreign yachts may be demanded.
>
> **Facilities.** Provisions and ice are to be obtained in the main square nearby; water at the quay. There is a bank, restaurants and a hotel.

The town, which formerly consisted of many three-storey houses with wrought-iron balconies, and was largely destroyed in the 1953 earthquake, has been subsequently rebuilt with modern shops and houses such as one might expect to find in other European countries. The large square with modern municipal buildings has also replaced earlier buildings set up during the governorship of Sir Charles Napier, whose statue is in London's Trafalgar Square. In Argostoli there was a predominant influence inherited from Venice as well as something from Britain; many prominent lawyers, doctors, shipowners and local country families intermarried with Venetians and lived in the Cephalonian capital. Byron came here with his staff in 1823 and resided in the town during the autumn months before departing for Mesalonghion to take a more active part in the War of Independence.

The Second World War was not a happy period for Argostoli. First occupied by the Italians who capitulated in 1943, the island was then invaded by German troops who, finding themselves outnumbered and lacking food, rounded up their late allies, drove them into camps and with automatic weapons shot the whole Italian garrison of more than 5,000 officers and men.

On the west side of this large gulf is the smaller Port Lixuri, reached from

Argostoli by ferry in half an hour. Following along the shore by the small promontory the ferry soon comes to a mill. This is only the reconstruction of the famous mill built by Mr Stevens, an Englishman, early in the last century. Its fame was due to the stream of water flowing from the sea which drove the corn-mill and then disappeared into a fissure in the rock, to emerge no-one knew where. Many visitors came to see this phenomenon, and some American scientists who tried to locate the eventual destination of the disappearing stream, met with no success. Then came the 1953 earthquake and all was destroyed. Recently the mill has again been set up, but this time worked by electric power to amuse tourists.

On the point of the promontory is Sir Charles Napier's lighthouse—a white rotunda supported by Ionic columns.

Lixuri, with 6,000 people, is of no particular interest; it has a small port with two breakwaters and 14-feet depths at the quays. Steamers load most of the currants here, but in strong south and east winds the quays are too exposed.

Port Assos is a small inlet on the west coast which has been much publicized by Greek Tourist Offices. Although attractive, Assos is hardly suitable as a summer anchorage; it is uncomfortably open to the north, whence a swell often rolls in.

Fiskardo Bay. An attractive inlet with suitable sheltered anchorage and a small village on the water-front.

> **Approach and Anchorage.** See Chart 720. One may enter by day or night and anchor in the northern corner of the inlet in 4 fathoms where there is just sufficient swinging room for a medium-sized yacht. Alternatively, a small yacht may berth stern to the southern quay among the fishing-boats where there is excellent shelter. The bottom is mud.
> **Facilities.** A water tap on the quay. Limited fresh provisions and ice by the bus from Argostoli. The Patras–Corfu ferry calls once a week in each direction.

The little anchorage has only limited space for yachts and the quays are usually monopolized by caiques working their cargoes. A new coastal road leads south towards Sami, a 4-hour drive in the bus; to Argostoli it is slightly more.

The present name of the place is derived from Robert Guiscard, known to the Italians as Viscardo, the successful Norman chieftain who died here in 1085 while leading his second expedition against the Greek Empire. Had he survived it is thought that he might well have forestalled the Latins and established a Norman dynasty in Constantinople and on the shores of the Bosporus and Black Sea.

Ayias Eufemia. A small village in a bay with a short, protecting pier; well-sheltered, except from the east.

> **Approach and Berth.** Chart 720. No officials. Anchor in 3 fathoms in the N.E. corner behind the mole, hauling in the yacht's stern to the quay where there are adequate depths for any size yacht, but caution is needed because the ballasting protrudes irregularly under water.
> **Facilities.** Water from a tap in the centre of the quay. General store in the village. A small summer hotel-restaurant and two tavernas. Bus communication with Sami and Argostoli. No sea communication.

It was from here that Byron, Trelawny and others made an excursion to Ithaca. On their return, according to Harold Nicolson, they visited the monastery of Moni Agrillion; it was an embarrassing occasion, for Byron, during an audience with the Abbott had one of his convulsive fits. The old monastery survived until the recent earthquakes, but now only a ruined bell-tower remains and only one monk to care for the modern replacement of the monastery. The ascent from Sami, with splendid views of the green mountainous country and other islands, is rewarding.

Sami. A newly constructed harbour among pleasant green mountains, but of no particular interest.

> **Approach.** Chart 720. *Sailing Directions* gives a good description. There is no difficulty day or night.
> **Berth.** Secure stern to the quay on the breakwater with bows south, where there are depths up to 3 fathoms near the bollards close to the ferry berths. Shelter is good, for the N.W. wind has only a short fetch. A small yacht can berth at the inner quay at the N.E. corner where there are 7-foot depths.
> **Officials.** Harbour, Customs and Immigration.
> **Facilities.** Fresh water can sometimes be obtained from a tap near the quay. Fuel and provisions can be bought nearby, and there are two small restaurants in the village on the waterfront. A taxi to Argostoli takes 45 minutes, and the occasional bus $1\frac{1}{2}$ hours. Ice must be brought from Argostoli, and water is often in short supply. There is no bank at Sami.

Four steamers call each week connecting with Corfu, Patras and Piraeus, and a car-ferry now plies twice daily connecting Sami with both Patras and Corfu. It berths at the extremity of the breakwater.

The whole village of Sami (1,200 people) was destroyed by earthquake in 1953 and has been completely rebuilt with British funds. Although an important link for car-ferry communications it is disappointing to find so few amenities. This port has largely replaced Argostoli (the capital) as the major port of call for passengers and car-ferries, and the recently improved roads have now assured the importance of Sami's commerical situation.

It was at Sami that the Christian fleet under Don John of Austria assembled immediately before the Battle of Lepanto. A few miles inland, and west of Sami, lies the recently discovered cave of Melissani with its underground river now approached by a flight of steps. Here one may pay a small fee and explore the recesses of the lake and river by boat. An interesting discovery was recently made by two Austrian professors that when a strong dye is poured into the water at the sea-mills of Argostoli it may be expected to emerge in the river water at Melissani some three weeks later.

If sailing northwards to pass through the Ithaca Channel, it should be borne in mind that a strong wind sets in from the north in the summer afternoons and is apt to come in gusts off the steep-to mountains.

Sailing southwards towards Cape Kapri one reaches the green Pronos Bay with the small and shallow port of Poros, adjoining some small hamlets and an impressive gorge leading to a green cultivated plain.

Poros. (See Chart 720.)

> **Approach and Berth.** The mole, which extends eastward for 120 yards, has a quay with 12-feet depths near its extremity (Lt. Fl. (G)). The shallow water allows only just room for a medium-sized yacht to lay out an anchor and berth stern-to. N.E. winds are not safe for vessels in the port.
> **Facilities** are few. No water, a general store—a small summer hotel, two tavernas.

A loading tip on the eastern arm of the bay belonged to a former mining company, now liquidated.

Proceeding southwards with the intention of rounding the bold Cape Mounda one should give a wide berth to the off-lying Kakkava shoal as the bottom here has risen appreciably and soundings shown on the chart are no longer accurate.

The Island of Zante (Zakinthos)

This island comes third in importance among the Ionian Islands after Corfu and Cephalonia. In ancient times it was praised by Strabo for the richness of its woods and harvests and more recently was known by the Italians as 'The Flower of the Levant'. From seaward the countryside seems hardly deserving of such praise, but when standing on the high ground looking down upon the great central plain one appreciates the rich green cultivation. There are splendid views across the plain towards the tall mountains beyond.

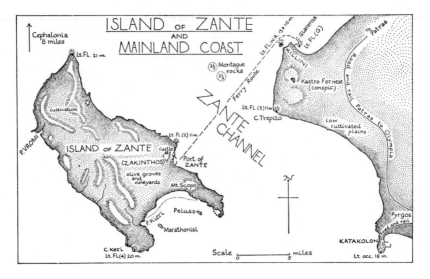

Port Zante. A spacious port with an attractive modern town surrounded by partially bare hills.

> **Approach and Berth.** Chart 720. The entrance is straightforward. Proceed close to the mole and berth beyond the projecting jetty, stern to quay and bows to the southward; anchor in $2\frac{1}{2}$ fathoms. The bottom is soft mud, but the holding appears adequate. Good shelter except in Sirocco (S.E.) winds when the harbour is very disturbed and a yacht must shift berth into the southern corner where getting ashore can be difficult.
>
> **Officials.** A Port of Entry. Port Authority and Customs.
>
> **Facilities.** Fresh water at the quay can be arranged by the Harbour Master. Diesel fuel is available at the quay and petrol at a garage in the town nearby. Good provision shops and a very palatable Zante wine (dry) is available on draught. Two or three good tavernas are near the quay and a new hotel on the water-front, as well as summer restaurants.
>
> In the summer, a car-ferry runs three times a day from Killini (Glarenza) on the mainland ($1\frac{1}{2}$ hours); there is also a daily air connection with Athens.

In the great earthquake of 1953 most of the old Venetian town was destroyed including the English Church of St John. The Venetian church of St Nicolas, however, survived as did many of the tombstones in the English cemetery. This is entered through the old wrought-iron gates beside the royal arms of Queen Victoria. There is almost nothing surviving today to mark the Venetian–British culture which had once happily blended with that of the well-to-do families of Zante. The modern town, reconstructed after the plan of the former Venetian one, accommodates about 13,000 people; its main square and public buildings especially are attractive. A museum houses some altar screens, frescoes and minor treasures from the wrecked churches.

Recently, extensive harbour improvements were made, including the dredging of the western side of the port and the rebuilding of the inner quays. This is to provide additional berthing space for small steamers, which lift considerable quantities of currants, gypsum, olive oil and lemons, upon which the island's prosperity depends.

The currants, mostly grown in the great plain, are produced from the dwarf vine. When the fruit is fully ripe it is gathered about August and spread out on levelled areas to dry for three weeks under the hot sun. Each estate has its own drying area, and often these colourful patches may be seen, especially on the high ground, a long way from seaward. Currants from Zante have been shipped to England since the sixteenth century, at which time they were also made into wine, and these currants were known in England long before the kitchen-garden shrub was introduced; the latter is unknown in Greece. The word currant is a corruption from the French *Raisins de Corinthe*.

Near the southern tip of the island one may anchor in

Port Kieri, a cove, open between N.E. and S.S.E. lying on the west side of Kieri Bay.

> **Anchorage** is near the end of a destroyed stone pier in the S.W. corner of the cove. The depths slowly decrease from 3 to 2 fathoms. Let go 70 yards S.E. of the pier's extremity, towards the high southern shore. Bottom is sand.
> **Facilities** are very limited. Only a bar, open in the tourist season, when bathing parties come out for the day. Possibly a little fruit and vegetables can be bought, and sometimes a locally produced Rosé wine.

There is no longer anything of interest to be seen. A pitch pool by the shore is no longer used, and there are others further inland shown on the chart. They were described by Herodotus (IV.195), but today the pitch is rarely used even on local boats. The land is cultivated; cattle are to be seen grazing and olive groves are maintained.

The whole west coast of Zante is inhospitable with steep-to white cliffs. The only possible shelter is at

Port Vromi, a very small creek with steep-to sides, open over a narrow arc to S.W. Local boats and very occasionally a small yacht has put in for the night during calms or offshore winds. There is only limited room to anchor, for the creek narrows and a warp must be run ashore. The place is entirely deserted. One would not like to be caught here in unsettled weather.

> **History.** Zante, like most of the Ionian Islands, suffered only a brief Turkish occupation, and when the Venetians came in the fifteenth century the island soon began to prosper. The

growing of olives and the currant trade began to thrive, and also the commerical port which, on account of the loss of Modon to the Turks, now became the main provisioning and watering base for the Venetian merchant ships trading with the East. The Pilgrim galleases and naval escorts also had to make use of Zante as a base. In Queen Elizabeth's reign, with the founding of the British Levant Company, merchant ships came here to load with currants, and also called here when routed to Levant ports. Many English merchants began to congregate in the town in pursuit of commercial interests, and their descendants continued to reside here until very recent years.

The British Navy has frequently been associated with Zante. After the Battle of the Nile, the inhabitants presented Nelson with a sword and cane; Codrington came here to provision his allied squadron immediately before the Battle of Navarino in 1827; and Abney Hastings, that great exponent on iron-ships and red-hot shell so successfully used against the Turks in the War of Independence, came here a year later, badly wounded on board *Karteria* where he died a few days later.

The Mainland Coast and Islets of the 'Inland Sea'—*See map, page 23*

The sheltered 'Inland Sea' lies between the line of large islands, just described, and the mountainous mainland coast. Following this coast southwards from the Levkas Canal no shelter will be found until reaching the vicinity of Dragamesti, some 25 miles distant, but at one or two of the islands passed en route there are some pleasant inlets with good anchorages described on page 28.

On the mainland coast are the following places:

Marathea Bay (Chart 1939) lying at the northern entrance to Dragamesti. Here, in mountainous surroundings one may anchor in 3-fathom depths at the head of this deserted bay.

Astakos (Chart 1939) lying at the head of the large Dragamesti Bay, is an uninteresting village overshadowed by Mount Veloutzi (3,000 feet). A long protecting mole and a quay provide good shelter and a berth off the yacht station. The village has a number of shops, and in addition to provisions, fuel and ice can be bought.

Pandelemona provides two anchorages in wild deserted surroundings:

(a) in the cove off some ruined houses suitable for shallow draught yachts;
(b) off the fork of two creeks in 5-fathom depths in good shelter and holding.

Plateali or **Platea** (Chart 3485) is more suitable as a fleet anchorage.

Kamaros Bay has a hamlet and a short mole with 2-fathom depths close off.
  After Plaka Bay, the Acarnanian Mountains give way to the swampy plain of the Aspro River.

Petala, the most southerly anchorage, is close to the entrance to the Gulf of Patras. There are depths here of 2 to 3 fathoms on a mud bottom with fine weed—good shelter and holding. At the head of the inlet, by the shallows, is a fishing settlement with many stakes and small boats.

Skrofa, opposite Oxia Island, is an isolated shallow inlet among the lagoons. Entrance is north of the islet, but very shallow, and scarcely suitable even for a small yacht. It is, however, of interest that on New Year's Day, 1824, Byron's *Mistico* (a fast lateen-rigged vessel with tall poop) bound for Missolonghi, was glad to put into this secluded little inlet to evade the pursuing Turkish gunboats.
  Proceeding southwards one soon enters the Gulf of Patras—*See Chapter 2.* The river water continues to bring down silt, thus extending the shallows and necessitating a vessel keeping a mile offshore. Interest in these waters was recently aroused following the discovery of certain narratives and detailed plans of the Battle of Lepanto. These had been stored away among the archives of the Knights of Malta and have now been brought to light in Valetta University library. During the final phase of the battle, the Turkish galleys, fleeing from the onslaught of the victorious Christian fleet, tried to escape destruction by making for the shallows. There are reasons for thinking that something of these galleys still remains hidden under the silt of four hundred years and it was encouraging to find, in the Autumn of 1971, that ubiquitous sea archaeologist Peter Throckmorton making a thorough survey of the sea-bed with modern sonar equipment.
  Of the nearby islets, the **Dragonera Group**, which is largely uninhabited, and the **Echinades** (named after the sea-urchin, because of their prickly outline) serve no useful purpose other than contributing to the beauty of the seascape.

History. The Battle of Lepanto, which took place on 6th October, 1571, was the last of the great galley actions ever fought, when the Christian States of Europe led by Don John of Austria (even younger than Alexander on his Asian campaign) gained a decisive victory over the Turks; not only did the combined fleet destroy the enemy forces, but they shattered the Turkish belief in their invincibility. Historians relate that about 250 galleys fought on either side, and they record that arrows, javelins, fireballs, cannon, muskets, spears and swords were used in this spirited action when at least 25,000 Turks were killed. Over 200 Turkish galleys were captured or sunk, and 15,000 Christian slaves, chained to their benches, were liberated. Among the casualties in Don John's fleet was Cervantes, who lost his left hand; with his right, some forty years later, he recorded *Don Quixote*. Trophies from the action may be seen among maritime collections in eastern Mediterranean ports; fine figure-heads and other emblems captured from Turkish galleys. In London, although it was a Catholic victory, 'there were bonfires made through the citie, with banqueting and great rejoicing'.

Though the galleys had fought their last major action they continued in the Mediterranean for another two centuries, their activity being limited to piracy. Their crews came mostly from Livorno, Algiers, Sicily and Malta; only in France were the galleys taken over by the Navy, and it was not until the Revolution that the remaining galley-slaves were at last freed.

> *And above the ships are palaces of brown*
> *black-bearded chiefs,*
> *And below the ships are prisons, where with*
> *multitudinous griefs*
> *Christian captives, sick and sunless, all a labouring*
> *race repines*
> *Like a race in sunken cities, like a nation in the mines.*
>
> G. K. CHESTERTON, *Lepanto.*

Immediately south of the Echinades, and forming a turning point for the Gulf of Patras, is

Oxia Island. Mountainous, steep-to and uninhabited, this relatively small island affords one anchorage which might be useful to a yacht. This is in the north and is suitable in settled weather.

Anchorage. Let go at the head of the cove in 3 to 4 fathoms with sufficient room to swing. The holding is good and the fetch to the north is about $1\frac{1}{4}$ miles.

On the west side of Oxia is another cove with precipitous sides, but the depths are too great for anchoring.

The Island of Ithaca, a general view

Looking towards Port Vathi

The mansion on Moudra Islet

The Island of Ithaca: Port Kioni

THE GULFS OF PATRAS AND CORINTH

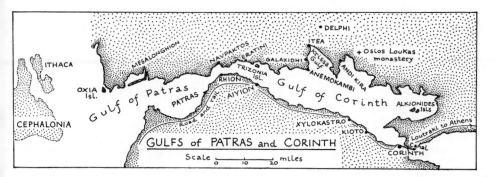

GULF OF PATRAS
  Mesalonghion (Missolonghi)
  Patras (Patre)
GULF OF CORINTH
Northern Shores
  Narrows of Rhion
  Navpaktos
  Eratini
  Trizonia Island
  Krissa Gulf
  Anemokambi (Andromaki)
  Galaxidhi
  Itea
  Salona Bay (Krissa)
  Andikira (Aspra Spitia)
  Kefali Peninsula
  Alkionides Islands.
  Loutraki
  Corinth and the Canal
Southern Shores
  Aiyion and minor anchorages.

2

The Gulfs of Patras and Corinth

THE GULF OF PATRAS

The Gulf of Patras is 13 miles wide at its mouth, where the shores are low; the northern side is shallow, with swamp water from the Aspro River. From the tall, rocky Oxia Island at the northern entrance it is 30 miles to Patras, a relatively large port, lying among green mountains near the head of the gulf.

Along the northern shores of the gulf suitable anchorage can be found in accordance with the fathom contours on the chart, and there is complete shelter at the small port of Mesalonghion approached by a 3-mile canal. On the south coast there is nowhere suitable.

In the summer months it is usually calm at night and in the forenoon, but towards mid-day a sea breeze sets in from the westward which can excite a small sea at the port of Patras. As one enters further into the gulf towards the Narrows of Rhion the mountainous scenery becomes magnificent.

A number of fishing craft are based at the low-lying creeks and at night their lamps create a dazzling impression over the waters of the gulf. In addition to usual sea fish, mullet, bream, sardines, there are turtles which may often be seen in early summer making their way into the lagoons.

In early spring and September, woodcock, snipe, duck and quail are shot both here and on the marshes near Lepanto and Drepano. In the country behind Patras there are a number of unfrequented ravines where plenty of redleg partridges may be found.

Mesalonghion or **Missolonghi.** An historic little town and port approached by a 3-mile canal.

> **Approach.** Chart 1676. Though the low swampy coast is difficult to discern, the buoys marking the southern end of the canal are large and well lit.
>
> The canal is marked by four pairs of beacons and is nearly 3 miles in length. The beacons are lit and sited 50 yards apart on the sides of the canal; but it is noted that the sides are very irregular and sometimes narrow from the official width of 50 yards to only 30 yards to less. Although the banks are marked by large beacons, the actual line of the bank may often be discerned by its discoloured water. There are depths of 3 fathoms in the channel all the way, except at the entrance which sometimes silts to just over two.

Berth. In the basin forming the port, there are 3-fathom depths with sufficient room to ride at anchor or haul in the stern to one of the quays. The port has been rebuilt with modern quays, and further swampland has been reclaimed. There is perfect shelter. To obviate a recurrence of malaria, the basin and lagoons are frequently sprayed from aircraft.

Several small coasters use the port, and it is claimed that vessels of 600 feet and 17-feet draught may be accommodated, although they would not always clear the bar.

Facilities. The town, with a population of 15,000 has been considerably improved in recent years, and on summer evenings people may be seen dining at tables around the main square, while a colourful fountain plays in the middle. A Xenia hotel was built, only to be closed a year later for lack of tourists, there are no shops close to the port, but it is only a 10-minute walk to the town. There is a water-tap at the N.E. corner of the basin. Beyond is a 'Garden of Heroes' with Byron's statue in the centre and that of Captain Abney Hastings in a prominent position. In the town square is a museum with a few relics of Byron.

Mesalonghion is famous for its gallantry during the early twenties of the last century when its defences against the invading Turkish army excited world interest in the Greek cause. It was also here, just before this event, that Byron had tried to rally the various Greek factions but died shortly after his thirty-seventh birthday.

Byron's original house on the shore of the lagoon was destroyed with the rest of the village when the Turks overran Mesalonghion in 1826. A year to two later, this and other dwellings were reconstructed on the same foundations, and so now an unattractive two-storey house reputed to be that of 'Veeron' is possibly much the same as the original building. It was here that Byron spent his last three unhappy months in the cause of Greece.

His mission had ended disastrously, most of his tasks being unfulfilled; moreover, his staff had failed him. The long chain of disappointments had taken a toll of his health; he wrote almost no poetry, although on his thirty-seventh birthday, with sudden inspiration, he composed 'the Sword, the Banner and the Shield'. Byron's few happy moments were on the occasions when he tore himself away from the frustration of office work. Paddling across the lagoon in his canoe, he would find a horse awaiting him and would then spend a few hours riding over the flat country, at that period clear of marauding Turks. Returning from one of these expeditions, a heavy rainstorm overtook him; soaked to the skin and chilled by the cold April wind he was soon seized with rheumatic pains. Already he had suffered from a 'stroke' and became delirious.

The four doctors, in whom he had little faith, resorted to bleeding, but his strength quickly waned and he died on 19th April, 1824. After an autopsy the body was embalmed, placed inside a tin-lined case, with 180 gallons of spirit in a large barrel. A small vessel took three days to sail it to Zante; as she sailed out into the lagoons, thirty-seven mourning guns were fired at minute intervals as a last tribute from the Greeks, who proclaimed national mourning for twenty-one days. The brig *Florida* then sailed with the body to London, where the English judged Byron differently: not only was an Abbey burial denied but neither bust nor plaque were placed in Poets' Corner until 145 years had passed. On 8th May, 1969, a stone memorial was dedicated.

Patras (Patrae or **Patre).** A medium-sized commercial port, capital of the Peloponnesus: the third largest city in Greece.

Approach and Berth. Chart 1676. This is easy day or night, but there is no convenient berth. The best place is near the southern end of the centre mole which is sheltered from N.E. winds which are often fresh in summer. Westerly winds which are more frequent can also cause inconvenience at this berth, in which case a yacht should shift to the north side of the mole. It is not a safe port in which to leave a yacht unattended, except in the early part of the day when it is usually calm, but in 1971 the detached mole was extended by 100 yards in a N.N.E. direction which should improve the shelter.

Caution. Beware of under-water boulders which have come away from the mole's foundations and endanger yachts berthed at the yacht station.

Local Officials. As necessary for a Port of Entry. A British Consul resides in the port.

Facilities. Provisions and limited yacht stores are available close at hand. There is a good fresh water tap on the jetty. Three or four hotels and some good restaurants are nearby. Two or three banks. Engine repairs can be undertaken. A ferry port for Corfu–Brindisi car-ferry, and for Cephalonia ferries. A motorway connects with Athens.

Entering Patras harbour, the beautiful view of the surrounding green mountains is obscured by the larger buildings of the town.

The port developed as a result of the currant trade before the last century. Usually one or two large freighters are working cargoes at the quays. The town of 95,000 people is uninspiring, but it lies conveniently on the Athens railroad, whose diesel trains also reach Olympia in $3\frac{1}{2}$ hours. The country around is beautiful and partly wooded, its rising slopes growing vines and oranges; the Claus wine factory is worth a visit. There are magnificent views from the Venetian castle above the town.

Built during the height of its commercial prosperity early in the last century on the grid system, the arcaded buildings on the water-front provide welcome shade from the hot sun. This, however, is the more agreeable part of the city; a wide main artery, leading inland, comes to a long flight of broad steps. Avenued by oleander shrubs in red and white, this stairway leads up to the only historical monument now remaining—the castle, almost entirely Venetian and mainly in good repair, standing on the spur of the hill.

The interest is not so much in the castle itself but in the view from the top which is the grandest in Greece. In the evening light it looks its best: the distant peaks of Zante and Cephalonia can be seen to the westward; on the northern side of the gulf is the tall Oxia Island; sweeping further towards the east are the lagoons of Mesalonghion and the two nearer, steep and rugged mountains of Varasov and Klovara; finally one sees the two fortresses guarding the Narrows of Rhion and the walls of the ancient city of Lepanto climbing the slopes behind.

History. Patras was the scene of the crucifixion of St Andrew, and many Greeks still believe that his remains lie beneath the high altar of their principal church. There is, however, certain interest to Scotsmen in the story of a Greek monk who during the fourth century, fearing a

47

Barbarian invasion, carried off the remains of the saint to Fifeshire, where subsequently a fine cathedral was built at St Andrews to perpetuate his memory. The Italians also claim to have at least some portions of the saint, for at the annual fiesta at Amalfi a large and colourful procession emerges from the cathedral of St Andrea bearing the treasured casquet they believe to contain the bones of St Andrew.

In more modern times the Greek Church played a prominent part here, for in 1821 the Bishop of Patras raised the flag of independence, an event of such patriotic significance that the incident was for many years portrayed in old-fashioned engravings in holy places until superseded by more recent pictures of Greek patriots repelling German parachutists, and other warlike scenes.

THE GULF OF CORINTH

Coming to the **Narrows of Rhion,** once known as the 'Little Dardanelles', one leaves the Gulf of Patras and enters the **Gulf of Corinth.** At the Narrows the width is a couple of miles and on either side lie the ruins of a low fortress, Turkish structures imposed upon military works of Venetians, Crusaders and earlier intruders. At the elbow-bend north of the port of Patras an appreciable current is sometimes whipped up suddenly by the wind, thus making progress through the Strait difficult without using power.

The well-sheltered ramps on each side of the Strait enable an efficient car-ferry service to operate across the Narrows.

The Gulf is 65 miles in length, with the Corinth Canal at its eastern end. The scenery on either side is mountainous: green slopes flanking the northern shores ascend Mount Parnassus—'Mother of surging streams'—and on the south are the tall ranges of the Peloponnesus. Whereas the northern shores are indented and provide shelter at a number of places, the southern coast is mostly straight and without protection.

The Wind in summer usually springs up freshly from the west about mid-day and dies away towards sunset. At night there is often a gentle breeze from the east which may continue until the forenoon. In unsettled conditions squalls may come off the mountains with considerable strength; but the more dangerous symptoms occur with humid easterly weather when the wind may do a volte-face and blow with great strength from the west. This may last a few hours or more and then suddenly cease:

> *Gone like a bird, like a blowing flame*
> *In one swift gust when all things are forgotten.*
> EURIPIDES

The Northern Shores

Navpaktos (Lepanto). A minute fishing port, rich in history, and worth a visit for the satisfaction of entering such an interesting old walled-in port.

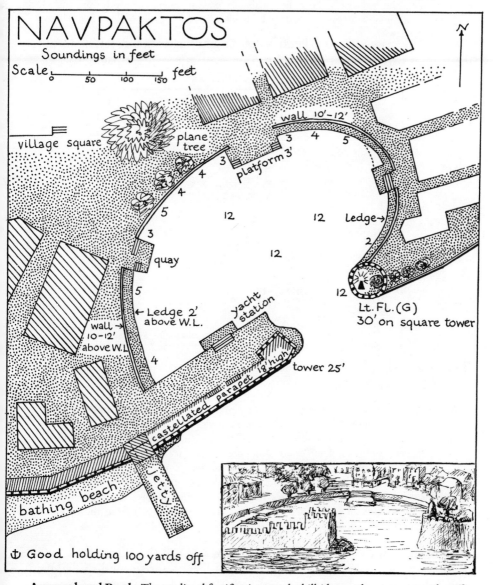

Approach and Berth. The medieval fortifications on the hillside may be seen some miles off. The opening in the old wall of the port is easy to discern.

The best shelter is obtained close under the western quay with anchor laid out east. The circular harbour is very small, being only 80 yards across.

Officials. The Harbour Master's office is above the berth mentioned.

Facilities. Fresh water, fuel and provisions are available. A modern restaurant is by the port. Of the medieval town only the walls remain. By walking along the top towards the clock tower a wonderful view may be had of the whole Gulf of Corinth.

It was at Lepanto that the Turkish fleet sought shelter before setting forth for the famous battle against the Christian states of Europe. (See page 41.)

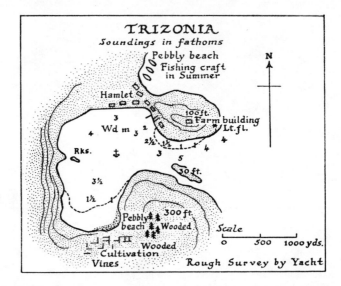

Trizonia Island. A very pleasant sheltered anchorage in a small island with a primitive hamlet.

Approach. Chart 1600. It is easy by day or night, but once inside the entrance of the bay, its northern shore should be given a berth of 80 yards.

Anchorage. There are convenient depths off the hamlet. The bottom is mud with a thin carpet of weed and the holding good. Being open to east, it is sometimes practical to anchor in this southern portion of the bay to gain better shelter.

The main village of Trizonia is on the mainland, half a mile across the strait; but on the island is the small hamlet which houses during the summer months a few fishermen and the peasants who cultivate corn, vines and olives. Fresh water, piped from the mainland, is available in the hamlet.

Looking northwards there is a lovely view towards the village on the mainland, where cypresses and grass-green vines form a foreground to the gently rising slopes carpeted sometimes with red oleander shrubs reaching towards the high Parnassus beyond.

Eratini is a small hamlet lining the water-front of a cove which affords good protection from the west winds.

Anchorage is about 70 yards off the beach in 5 to 7 fathoms with good holding; a slight swell rolls in during strong winds.

Facilities. Bread and vegetables can be bought. A bus runs daily to Amphissa and a caique crosses to Aiyon on the Peloponnesus.

The surrounding country produces olives and barley, also market garden produce.

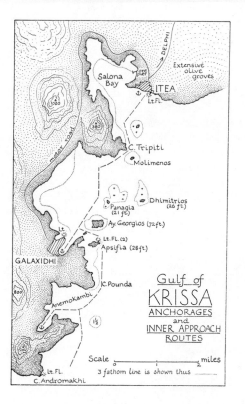

Krissa Gulf (Krissaios Kolpos)

Chart 221. Known until recently as Salona Bay, is the most interesting part of the Gulf of Corinth for a yacht to visit. On the western shores at the entrance lies the deserted cove of Anemokambi, then comes the pleasant little port of Galaxidhi; towards the head of the gulf, the commercial port of Itea (a necessary call for visiting Delphi). Salona, the former name for the bay at the head of this gulf is of interest only on account of a spirited naval action which took place during the War of Independence. (See page 54.)

Anemokambi (or sometimes **Andromaki**). A small creek in complete isolation with all-round shelter. A convenient night anchorage half-way along the Gulf of Corinth.

Approach. Charts 1600 and 221. Easy by day, but the position of the off-lying shoal (10 feet) four cables east of Cape Traklos should be kept in mind.

Anchorage. About 100 yards from the head of the creek is a depth of $2\frac{1}{2}$ fathoms with a bottom of soft mud.

The country around grows some crops and there are one or two peasant cottages in the distance, otherwise solitude.

Galaxidhi. A pleasant, sheltered cove suitable for yachts visiting Delphi. The village lines the water-front of the S.E. cove.

Approach. Charts 1600 and 221. By day the islands are easy to discern and there is no difficulty in entering the inlet with an attractive pinewood on its S.E. side. For those without the large-scale chart the following direction may be useful:

It is unnecessary for a medium-sized yacht to follow *Sailing Directions* for the deep-water route.

On leaving Anemokambi steer north-eastwards to round Cape Pounda, and then lay a course towards the islets of Apsifia and Ayios Georgios (which first appear as one island). After passing between them head N.W. to pass northward of the low islet of Petales (surmounted by a white stone beacon). It marks the end of the spit extending N.E. of the eastern headland of the port; from here one may safely steer into the entrance.

Anchorage. The quays were rebuilt in 1971, but when berthing stern-to one should beware of the under-water ballasting which protrudes irregularly. There are depths of 10 to 12 feet close beyond the former ferry-pier; this provides protection from the mountain squalls which often blow suddenly from the north. It is sometimes recommended to moor head and stern in the middle of the cove. Under certain unusual weather conditions phenomenal tidal waves, similar to those in certain Sicilian and Spanish bays, have been experienced here; the safety of a yacht when moored to the quay under these conditions is precarious.

Facilities. Limited provisions to be bought. Ice is available. Poor quality water from a tap near stone-pier. Two or three inferior restaurants and small summer hotels. A bus service, which has replaced the ferry, runs to Itea several times a day—20 minutes. It connects with buses to Delphi.

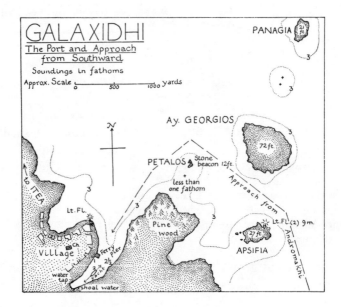

The village, now of little significance, lies opposite a pinewood on the other side of the bay. In a modest little museum are exhibited some relics from ships, and a few paintings which illustrate the importance of the place during its prosperity as a maritime centre more than a century ago.

History. When the War of Independence started, Galaxidhi, like Hydra and Spetsai, had a useful trading fleet of its own. In 1821, when the Turkish squadron set out to plunder Greek shipping there were sixty vessels at Galaxidhi. The Turkish admiral returned to Constantinople with thirty-five of them in tow and thirty prisoners hanging from the yard-arms of his flagship.

Itea. An unattractive town with an unsheltered roadstead used by steamers for embarking iron ore and olive oil. It may be worth a call if visiting Delphi, though in this case Galaxidhi as an alternative port is a pleasanter place to berth.

Approach. Chart 221 and *Sailing Directions* make the approach instructions clear for entry by day or night.
Berth. Secure the stern to the west side of the stone pier with anchor to the westward. There is good holding, and a depth of 2 fathoms at the pierhead for a distance of 70 yards along. Diesel fuel and petrol are available.
Officials. A Port of Entry. Harbour and Customs Immigration authorities.
Facilities. The town has 2,000 inhabitants mostly employed in small factories or in dealing with exports by sea and land. Steamers, which berth at the pier, ship minerals and iron ore. Fresh water, which is good, is laid on to the pierhead. There are some mediocre restaurants; tinned and fresh provisions can be bought. Petrol may be obtained from a pump in the street near the pier, and diesel fuel on the quay. A car-ferry plies to Aiyion.

Ancient Delphi is 20 kilometres along a good, well-graded road at an altitude of 2,000 feet. Perhaps the finest classical site in all Greece, Delphi, described in detail in many books, has several good hotels and can be reached in 40 minutes by taxi, or by bus in an hour.

The hinterland of Itea, the mouth of the gorge of Pleistos, is a mass of olive-groves. The ubiquitous culture of olives in the eastern Mediterranean, although perhaps no longer a matter of life and death, is still the most important factor in the nourishment of the people. It takes the place of butter and fats, and is the means of cooking—its ill-effect on the stomachs of newcomers from the west is often apparent.

The trees, usually cultivated in large groves of about twenty trees to the acre, are often seen from seaward standing well above sea level yet comfortably sheltered below the top of the ridge. They are said to prefer calcarious soil, and according to Pliny a rich soil often causes disease and a poorer quality of oil. Normally each tree may yield a quart of oil, which a robust man often consumes in little more than a week.

In antiquity the olive was the symbol of an age of fatness and fruitfulness. Its culture probably originated in Syria, the species being brought to Greece, Italy, Spain and France by Phoenician merchants. Athens, according to Herodotus, was the centre of the Greek olive industry. So important was a plentiful crop for the nation's survival that people were sometimes awed by the threat of prolonged periods of the N.E. wind and its ill effects: one may see today on the Tower of the Winds at Athens the symbol adopted for north-easterly weather—the figure of an elderly man spilling olives from his charger.

There is bus communication with Amphissia (with its Frankish castle) and with Athens (5 hours).

Salona Bay (Krissa) lies at the N.W. extremity of the gulf and though of no interest to a yacht today was once the scene of a spirited action.

On 29th September, 1826, the iron corvette paddle-steamer *Karteria* commanded by Captain Abney Hastings, led a small Greek squadron consisting of a brig and two gunboats

Karteria

into the bay. Here at anchor was a Turkish force consisting of an Algerine schooner, six brigs and two transports. Hastings anchored 500 yards off the nearest enemy ship which then opened fire. Hastings did the same, but with deliberate ranging shot, followed by hot shell from the long guns and 'carcass-shells' from the carronades. (His preference for hot shell rather than shot was because it was feared the solid shot might penetrate both sides of the enemy ships without doing much damage within.)

The effect of *Karteria*'s fire was terrific. The magazine of the Commodore's ship blew up; another carcass-shell exploded in the bows of a brig which began to sink; the Algerine was so damaged between-decks that she had to be abandoned; and more hot-shell set on fire two of the other brigs.

This successful action was considered to be the earliest effective proof of the superiority of an iron-ship, steam propulsion, and hot projectiles fired from large guns.

Continuing Eastward a number of sheltered anchorages are found with rather deep water and therefore more suitable for larger vessels. The chart reveals an occasional projection of sand or mud brought down by mountain torrents and suitable in emergency as a yacht anchorage. For the most part these bays have no interest. One place is worthy of mention:

Andikira (Aspra Spitia). An anchorage by a primitive village, on the shore of a deep mountainous gulf; more suitable for a large vessel.

> **Approach and Anchorage.** Chart 1600. The lighthouse in the approach is difficult to see by day; there are now lights on Cape Mounda and Tsaruchi Point.
> Anchor in 4 or 5 fathoms close off the village and take a line ashore to a post. There are no quays. In the anchorage the water is very deep. The S.W. corner of the bay should be avoided on account of the mooring buoys for the steamers which come to load bauxite.
> **Officials.** Harbour Master and Customs Officer.
> **Facilities** are very few, there being only a few shops and cafes.

A few yachts come here for the purpose of visiting Osios Loukas, 20 kilometres by taxi. There is, however, a more pleasant place to anchor for the night: an unnamed cove on the west side of the **Kefali Peninsula**. When anchored in its northern arm one has the impression of being landlocked; both the depths and nature of the bottom are suitable for a shallow draught yacht.

The surrounding mountain scenery is impressive—the Byzantine monastery of Osios Loukas standing close under Mount Loukas (1,600 feet) is 20 kilometres distant from Andikira and can be reached by taxi.

Alkionides Islands, lying 8 miles N.E. of Melangair Point, consist of two islands, largely barren, with two partially occupied monasteries.

> **Approach.** The islands can be recognized from afar by the conspicuous white monastery on the hillside. It would appear from the chart that, when approaching from the north, one would find suitable anchorage between the two islands. This is not so, for the channel shelves suddenly to a depth of only 3 feet at the Narrows, and the holding here is poor.
> **Anchorage.** Make for the southern shore of eastern island where a cove will be found near a small monastery surrounded by eucalyptus trees. In the centre of the cove are depths of 4 fathoms on a bottom of thin weed on mud. Although open between S.S.E. and S.W. (a 2-mile fetch) the cove is sheltered from the N.E. day breeze.

The monasteries appear to be occupied only during the summer months when some work on cultivation is carried out. Formerly called Kala Nisia (the Beautiful Isles) they apparently had many visitors some years ago.

Loutraki. A modern watering-place with a short mole affording limited protection from west. Loutraki is a convenient place to bring up for the night in calm weather when waiting to pass through the Corinth Canal.

Berth. Anchor towards east and stern to the mole—holding uncertain with large boulders. In fresh westerly winds a yacht should seek shelter at Corinth. A weak red light is sometimes exhibited at the extremity of the mole.

Facilities. Plenty of shops, provisions, hotels and restaurants. Bus service to Athens and tours to the Peloponnesus.

Certain historical sites can be conveniently visited from Loutraki:

Mycenae may be reached by bus, via Corinth, in about 2 hours. Buses leave for Corinth every hour.

Perakhora, a mountain village N.W. of Loutraki, may be reached by car in 20 minutes (or by the bus); it is an attractive drive through green hilly country. The Herain excavations lie towards Melangair Point, where there is a shallow bay approachable by small caique only.

Athens is about 2 hours' distant by train or bus.

> *Many a vanish'd year and age,*
> *And tempest's breath, and battle rage,*
> *Have swept o'er Corinth.*
> BYRON, *The Siege of Corinth*

Corinth. Chart 1600. The new harbour protected by a breakwater from westerly winds lies beside the uninteresting modern town.

Berth. In fine weather berth stern to the quay off the yacht station. If the wind should reach Force 6, it is best to cast off from the quay and ride to an anchor; the holding is good, firm mud. With strong westerly winds the seas surmount the breakwater and one should not anchor too close to it. In event of the wind veering to N.E. and becoming fresh to strong it is advisable to seek shelter off the shore S.E. of Loutraki.

Facilities. Water and fuel are available. Shops are a few minutes' walk, also some restaurants and tavernas. Expeditions to Akrocorinth, the ruins at old Corinth and many ancient sites on the Peloponnesus. Fast bus service to Athens.

Of the famous ancient Greek city of Corinth, little now remains. According to Thucydides, the Peloponnesian war of 431 B.C. was largely brought about by the jealousy between Corinth and Athens. Later destroyed by the Romans, Corinth was then rebuilt as their own city, becoming rich and luxurious at the time of Julius Caesar; it is mostly the ruins of this city which may be seen today. American archaeologists began to excavate at the end of the last century and one of their more spectacular achievements is the restoration of the theatre. Originally built in the fifth century B.C. to seat 18,000 people, it was rebuilt in marble by the Romans. In it they incorporated a special box for the emperor Nero. Nearby an inscription was found substantiating the famous story of the gladiator Androcles and the lion; it describes the occasion when Androcles' life had been spared due to the lion's timely recognition of the benefactor who had once extracted a thorn from his paw. The theatre is only one of many Roman remains excavated by the Americans; this ancient city is well worth a visit.

The ancient port of Lechaeum lies 3 miles west of the present port and was connected by high walls protecting a road leading directly up to the city. The largely silted entrance, difficult to discern from seawards, lies near the recently restored basilica; but it is disappointing to find that the inner port has become an area of black, reedy lagoons where only two quays and the canal can now be traced.

St Paul, who spent more than eighteen months here, was, on one occasion, brought for trial before the Roman consul; but 'Gallio cared for none of these things.' He subsequently wrote of the need for charity among the citizens of this wealthy commercial city and contrasted their materialism with a better world to come.

On Akrocorinth is perched the ruined medieval castle with extensive 17th-century Venetian walls surrounding the summit of the rock. Standing 1,800 feet about the sea, it affords a fine view across the Gulf of Corinth, and over the Saronic Gulf to Cape Sounion. Traces of walls date from the sixth century B.C., but most of those standing today are of medieval construction. Once occupied by Roger II, Norman King of Sicily, the citadel has changed hands many times, and on one occasion it was unsuccessfully attacked by the Knights of St John.

John d'Heredia, a French knight, became Grand Master of the Order of St John in Rhodes in 1376. A year later he set out with a squadron of nine galleys to attack the Turks, accompanied by the Priors of England: Robert Hales, St Gilles and Rome. After joining a Venetian fleet off Crete they made for Patras which they captured; but their attack on Corinth was an utter failure, and d'Heredia was taken prisoner.

The three priors promptly offered themselves as hostages to the Turks for the ransom of the Grand Master if they would release him. But d'Heredia refused to allow the sacrifice to be made because he thought the Order 'could more easily spare an old man like himself than three young and vigorous knights.'

The Corinth Canal, little over 3 miles in length, was cut by a French company towards the end of the last century. The saving in distance by vessels proceeding to Piraeus from, say, the direction of Brindisi is almost 130 miles, and the canal is used by many small steamers and caiques. Since vessels cannot pass one another in the canal they may have to wait outside until the blue burgee is hoisted to signify that the canal is clear and they may then enter.

The soft stone surface of the canal's vertical sides crumbles away and is continually under repair which often necessitates the canal being closed to traffic on a Sunday.

History. Before the construction of the canal, the Austro-Lloyd Steamship Company, which at the end of the last century had the monopoly of the Aegean and Levant trade, had to land its passengers at Loutraki, and then transport them by road to a steamer awaiting them on the Aegean side of the isthmus. However, the need for a canal was realized nineteen centuries before when the Emperor Caligula caused surveys to be made, and Nero actually initiated the diggings; but troublesome times brought the undertaking to nothing.

Meanwhile, although heavy ships could not be transported across the isthmus, the more easily handled galleys could, and for many centuries were hauled across on rollers. Only very recently was unearthed, a section of this *diolkos* or limestone-paved roadway; it is 14 feet wide and the two ruts which bore the rollers are 5 feet apart. History records that Augustus after the Battle of Actium had his ships dragged across the isthmus when in pursuit of Antony. In A.D. 883 the Greek admiral also had his fleet dragged across when he was preparing to repel the Saracens.

The Passage of Yachts through the Canal. On her first entry into Greece from abroad a small yacht pays the minimum dues of about £1.50 sterling, payable in any currency. Thereafter for every subsequent passage she pays the minimum of 103 drachmas so long as she remains in Greek waters (1971).

THE GULF OF CORINTH—SOUTHERN SHORES

Following the Peloponnesian coast westward from Corinth one notices that it is well populated with a number of villages, large and small. The coastline is comparatively straight and the few minor indentations afford little shelter for a yacht.

One or two places with sandy beaches have recently become summer resorts, and in some cases a short mole has been built to allow local ferry boats to call; at Vrakhate and Kioto a yacht may find protection from the short sea or swell; at other places small trading stations have sprung up where caiques call for shipments of grapes, olives and lemons.

The coastal road and railway from Athens to Patras follow close to the shore, frequently crossing the torrent-beds which, after the rains, convey the flood water into the gulf. The new motor-way cuts mostly inland.

The mountain of Spira (with its monastery) 3 miles west of Xylokastro is easy to discern, and further westward is the steep Vourikos gorge leading from Dhiakopto to Kalavryta, a picturesque site with a shrine marking the spot where Bishop Germanus raised the standard of revolt at the beginning of the

War of Independence. A railway and track have been made to encourage tourists to visit not only the revered site of the bishop's patriotic stand but the famous monastery of Megaspelaeon, best visited by road from Patras. This is a remarkable pile of white buildings standing one above the other let into the steep-to face of a huge limestone cliff. Above all stands the monastery church recessed into a large cavern. There is nothing special to be seen within, as the whole place was last burnt down in 1949 and rebuilt; the main interest lies in the history of the monastery's successful defence in 1826 against a large force of Turks under Ibrahim Pasha.

Apart from Corinth and the Canal the only port on the south shore is **Aiyion** (Chart 1676 with plan), an industrial town of 15,000 people. The Itea ferry berths behind its breakwater and in the autumn months small steamers, that lift the currants grown in the hinterland, berth here too. The only reason for a yacht to call here would be for the good fresh water (once praised by Pausanius) available at the jetty.

Delphi, the Tholos

Navpaktos, entrance to the medieval port

The Island of Kithera: Kapsali Bay on the right

THE WESTERN SHORES OF THE PELOPONNESUS

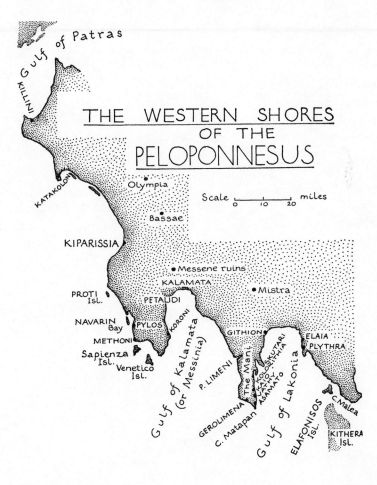

THE WESTERN SHORES
OF THE
PELOPONNESUS

Killini (Glarenza)
Katakolon
Kiparissia
Proti Island
Navarin Bay (Navarino)
  Pylos
Methoni
Sapienza Island
  Port Longos
Venetico Island
Gulf of Kalamata (Messinia)
Koroni
Petalidhi
Kalamata (Kalamon)
The Mani
Port Limeni
Gerolimena
Cape Matapan
  (Entrance to the Underworld)

Gulf of Lakonia
Asamato Cove
Port Vathi
Port Kaio
Kolokithia Bay Anchorages
  Meligani
  Solitare
  Nymphi
  Kotronas
  Skutari Bay
Githion (Yithion)
Elaia
Plythra
Elafonisos Island
  with Elli Islet anchorage
Vatica Bay
Vrakhonisos Petri
Neapolis
Cape Malea

3

The Western Shores of the Peloponnesus

Twenty miles from the entrance to the Gulf of Patras along a dull, low sandy coast is the small shallow port of Killini. Ten miles southward is the much better protected port of Katakolon, while 45 miles further still is Navarin Bay, well protected and interesting to visit. On the south-west coast, the only secure port is Kalamata in the Gulf of Messinia. Most of the places described provide temporary shelter during fine weather in the summer months.

Killini or **Glarenza,** a sheltered though decayed little Venetian port, is not safe in unsettled weather.

> **Approach.** See *Sailing Directions* and Chart 203. The breakwater has been largely breached by the winter gales, and its extremity, now under water, is marked by a conical light buoy.
> **Anchorage.** There are depths of 5 fathoms near the buoy and about 2 fathoms towards the root of the mole where dredging has taken place to accommodate the Zante ferries. Towards the destroyed part of the mole the depths decrease to 1 fathom. A yacht should anchor near the fishing craft berths in 2 fathoms; thin weed on sand. New quays, mainly for the Zante ferries, were completing in 1971; possibly future berths for yachts may be made available here.
> With a northerly wind a swell enters the port through the apertures in the mole.
> **Facilities** are very limited. There is a slow branch line which joins the main line from Patras to Olympia. A regular car-ferry service operates to Zante.

A car may be hired from a neighbouring village for the drive to Olympia, a journey of $1\frac{1}{2}$ hours.

An outstanding landmark, the Castle of Kelmutsi or Clermont (Krasto Tornese on the chart), is visible from the high land of Zante. It stands on the hill overlooking the harbour that was once the port for Genoese and Venetian trading vessels; it was then named Glarenza after the Duc de Clarence.

Begun in 1219, the castle was intended for protecting the coastal road from Corinth to Kalamata and Amdravida (the Frankish capital), and to ensure the safety of the port. Though smaller than some of the Syrian castles, this is considered the best example of a Frankish castle in the Morea. It was last used as a defence post during the War of Independence, when its Greek garrison was overcome by a Turco–Egyptian force under Ibrahim Pasha.

Katakolon, a small, safe, but uninspiring, commercial port.

Approach. Plan on Chart 719 shows that entry is easy by day or night. Within the harbour improvements have recently been made in the S.W. corner: the existing quay has had the depths increased to accommodate small steamers, and a substantial stone pier extends for 220 yards towards the molehead with depths of $3\frac{1}{2}$ fathoms at its extremity and alongside.

Berth. In strong winds a yacht should anchor off the new pierhead on a bottom of blue clay: excellent holding—under normal conditions the stern can be hauled towards the end of the pier with anchor to the eastward. In strong southerly winds a short swell of little consequence enters the harbour.

Port Facilities. The village, a miserable place with 1,000 inhabitants, has little to offer except a good taverna and a bakery. There is no fuel or water easily available. The nearest town is Pyrgos, 12 minutes by car and half an hour by train. Occasional passenger ferries call here in summer.

Officials. A Port of Entry. Customs and Harbour Authority.

The port receives over 200 small to medium-sized steamers in the year, mainly lifting currants grown in the interior. It is surprising to find such a wretched place where the port trade appears to be improving.

A taxi may be obtained to drive to Olympia (45 minutes) or one can go by bus via Pyrgos in $1\frac{1}{2}$ hours. The drive to the Doric temple at Bassae, passing through beautiful country, takes 3 hours by taxi.

The Gulf of Arcadia or Kiparissia, a 30 miles sweep of open sandy coast, affords temporary shelter.

Kiparissia, an open anchorage protected by a 300 yard mole. Chart 719 gives a plan showing detail of the shallow anchorage.

Kiparissia, once the harbour for Messene, was known in the Middle Ages as Arcadia on account of the refugees who fled from Arcadia because of the Slav invasion. Although its harbour was a busy place in Byzantine days when the defences were strengthened, the present port is of no interest today. The upper village, however, is attractive; its winding streets, flights of steps and a Turkish fountain make a visit worth while.

Proti Channel has an indifferent anchorage under the island as shown on Chart 719. Navarino, so very much better, lies only 5 miles to the southward.

About 4 miles north of the entrance to Pylos is 'Port' **Voidhkoilia,** shown on a large scale on Chart 211. Weather permitting this can be used as temporary anchorage for visiting Nestor's Cave and the ruined fortress of Paleo Averino, which are difficult of access by land. This is a perfect bay for bathing. It is open to winds between north and south but is partially sheltered by a small island. There are depths of 2 fathoms just behind the island, but there is certainly no port today.

Navarin Bay (Navarino),★ 50 miles south of Katakolon, is a large bay easy of access in bad weather; with its small sheltered port of **Pylos**, the place is also of wide historical interest.

> *Old man, go tell the wise Penelope*
> *That safe from Pylos I have sailed the deep.*
>
> Odyssey, XVI.16.

Approach and Berth. On entering the Bay, head for the extremity of Pylos breakwater—no difficulty day or night. Now turn into the port and lay out anchor to S.E. hauling in the stern to the mole. With easterly gales strong gusts sweep down the hilly slopes, but the holding is good and the sea undisturbed. Only with S.W. gales is there a swell.

Facilities. There is a fresh-water tap near the extremity of the mole; a number of fresh provision shops, one or two buses and restaurants and one or two modern hotels. There is bus communication with Athens.

Officials. As for Port of Entry.

Navarin Bay is sometimes used by British liners embarking Greek emigrants for Australia; they are brought to Pylos by road from Athens.

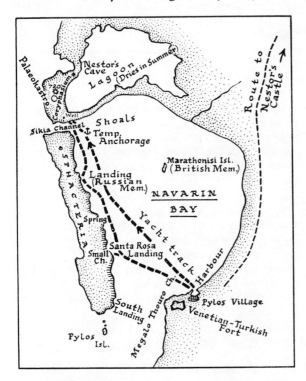

History. The earliest historical occasion recounted by Thucydides was the 'Sphacteria incident' in 425 B.C., when a small Athenian naval contingent under Demosthenes eventually overwhelmed a besieging force of Spartans.

To investigate the scene of this early operation, one must proceed to the sandy shore close to the shallow Sikia channel, and anchor off the ancient port of Coryphasium, whose mole can still be discerned disappearing among rushes into the sand. From here a mule track ascends the 700-foot hill to the fortress on Palaeokastro. This was where Demosthenes had detached himself from the Athenian expeditionary force bound for Syracuse, and having seized this peninsula with half a dozen triremes, set

★ From Navarin Bay as far as Crete has been described in *The Aegean* and therefore, pilotage instructions are of necessity duplicated for this part of the coast.

himself up for the summer months to defy the besieging Spartans. Standing on the top one now looks down on the shallow channel where Demosthenes had once sheltered his triremes.

The existing fortress is of medieval construction, with battlemented walls in good preservation, and from here there is a magnificent view across the large semi-circular bay of Navarin towards the green undulating country beyond.

Descending the steep northern slope, one soon comes to the stalactite cave where Hermes was reputed to have hidden the cattle he had stolen from Apollo. It is known as Nestor's Cave. Inside, when the cloud of bats has scattered, the glistening sides become visible, lit by a shaft of light from a hole high up in the domed roof. From here the side of the dried-up salt lake must be followed to re-embark in the dinghy.

Crossing to the island, one realizes that the depths are too great for a yacht to anchor off the steep cliffs of Sphacteria; the only way is to land by dinghy at 'Russian Cove' while the yacht is anchored elsewhere. A rough track ascends to the most northerly of the three peaks, which had been the Spartan stronghold until the return of the Athenian fleet from Syracuse. Then the tables were turned and the besiegers became the besieged. Demosthenes effected a landing, cut off Spartan supplies and eventually forced the surviving garrison to surrender. This dramatic and decisive conclusion to the campaign was never forgotten by the Athenians, and for six centuries the Spartan shields were exhibited at Athens. On the hilltop today is merely the ruin of a small fort; but it is the setting that brings to life the events of the narrative so vividly told by Thucydides. In 1827 an equally dramatic event took place which led to Greece obtaining her independence.

The Turkish–Egyptian army was occupying the Peloponnesus and a fleet of 82 warships ranged in three lines, lay at anchor in Navarin Bay.

At 1.30 p.m. on 20th October Admiral Codrington led an allied fleet, including French and Russian squadrons, into the bay without any opposition from the Turkish batteries. Firing began when certain Turkish ships started shooting at British ships' boats. Immediately Codrington's fleet opened fire on the Turks and, fighting fiercely, they continued the action all day and during the night. During the darkness many Turkish ships could be seen bursting into flames, and when daylight came only 29 of the original 82 remained afloat. The damage and casualties among allied ships was extensive; although no ships were lost, considerable repairs had to be made good at Malta.

England and Turkey were not at war, nor did this 'untoward event'—an expression used in the King's speech in Parliament—cause them to declare war. Although people in England celebrated this battle as a great and glorious victory, few realized how poor the efficiency of British gunnery had become—only twenty-two years after Trafalgar: H.M.S. *Genoa*'s First Lieutenant giving evidence at a subsequent court martial, stated that the enemy was so close that he could plainly see the whites of their eyes, yet *Genoa* battered her opponent for two hours without diverging from a parallel position, both ships being at anchor. It is perhaps significant that the Navy's first gunnery school, H.M.S. *Excellent*, was established five years later.

To the Greeks, whose liberation was achieved largely as a result of this far-reaching event, this bore out the philosophy expressed by Euripides:

> *There be many shapes of mystery*
> *And many things God makes to be,*
> *Past hope or fear.*

And the end men looked for cometh not,
And a path is there where no man thought;
So hath it fallen here.

In the square of Pylos is an impressive memorial, with busts of Codrington and his allied Admirals; on the island of Sphacteria, at Panagoulas, and on the small islet of Marathonisi (Chelonaki), are small obelisks or modern plaques to commemorate the dead sailors of the French, Russian and British fleets respectively.

Salvage of the Sunken Fleet. Much gold and valuable jewels were believed to have been sunk in the Egyptian flagship.

Wedges of gold, great anchors, heaps of pearl
Inestimable stones, unvalued jewels,
all scattered in the bottom of the sea:
SHAKESPEARE, *King Richard III,*
Act I, Scene IV

Treasure-seekers have made repeated attempts to work on the sunken ships now lying in more than 20-fathom depths. The wrecks are largely buried in mud; in recent years Peter Throckmorton, the American archaeologist and diver, reported finding eight hulls with only their frames protruding above the soft mud. Further investigation is expected.

Apart from a well-preserved Turkish fort at the entrance to the bay, there is one further ancient site that should not be missed. This is Nestor's Palace of about 1200 B.C., whose excavation has only recently been completed by Professor Blegen; a great number of Linear B tablets were discovered here.

Eight miles southward from Navarino is the south-westerly point of the Peloponnesus with the remains of a Venetian port behind it.

Methoni (until this century called Modon) has a shallow bay, inadequately protected by a breakwater, with a modern village close by. A massive Venetian fortress jutting into the sea dominates the port.

Approach and Berth. Charts 207 and 719 show there are no difficulties day or night. After rounding the extremity of the breakwater the sea-bed rises very quickly. The most conspicuous object by day, not clear on the chart, is the large Turkish tower on the southern point of the fortress. In fair weather only, a yacht may berth stern to the small quay 20 yards inside the mole with anchor laid out to the northward; the depths here are 10 feet—it may be preferable to anchor off, with the same shelter, in 2½ fathoms where there is good holding

67

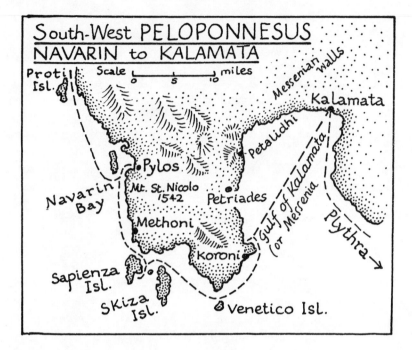

South-West PELOPONNESUS
NAVARIN to KALAMATA

and sufficient swinging room. The bottom is thin weed on sand and there are a few stones. A swell works round the end of the mole and in bad weather from the south the place is untenable.

In order to land at the castle or approach the village, one has to walk along the very rough 150-yard mole.

Facilities. Fresh water and fuel are laid on to a small quay near the molehead. The village has little character. A small hotel and a café are on the sea-front overlooking the sandy bay, which in summer attracts visitors. The road leads to Pylos and thence to Athens which can be reached by bus in 8 hours. Very few vessels call here, and only three or four fishing craft are based on the port.

The vast Venetian fortress is of limited interest, for within the walls hardly a building remains. The last time it was effectively used was in 1770 when the Russian fleet had based itself at Navarin. The fortress, then garrisoned by a strong force of Turks, constituted a threat to Russian supplies arriving by land and the Russian navy decided to capture it. An expedition supported by eighteen 24-pounders manned by Russian sailors from the fleet, together with 2,000 Greeks, failed to dislodge the garrison which was eventually relieved by a force of 6,000 Turks. Modon continued as a thorn in the flesh to the Navarin base until finally the Russians were compelled to abandon it.

In Venetian days, when it was known as Modon, this was one of the 'Eyes of the Republic', and because of its strategic position, it became a relatively large port. It lasted until the Peloponnesus was overrun by the Turks early in the 16th century.

From the top of the Adriatic where 'Venice sat in state, throned on her hundred isles', the pilgrim galleys made annual voyages to the Holy Land. Under oars and sail the state-owned galleys used to leave Venice every spring, laden with cargo and carrying pilgrims; they were escorted southwards by vessels of the Venetian Navy. Proceeding down the Italian coast and making calls as necessary, they put in at Brindisi and then crossed to Corfu for water and provisions. Thence southwards to Modon, calling here for replenishments and to rest the rowers. Subsequently they called at Hania in Crete, at Rhodes and at Cyprus before making their destination at Acre on the Palestine coast.

> *Pray for the pilgrims who fare by sea or overland that*
> *God may lead them forth and lead them in all safety*
> *of their bodies and souls.*

From one of the early prayers of the Knights of St John

On the cape pointing S.S.E. towards Sapienza Island is a prominent tower.

Protecting Methoni is the **Island of Sapienza,** which, in the sailing-ship days, provided a useful anchorage for vessels bound for the Aegean.

Port Longos provides anchorage for medium-sized vessels in southerly and westerly weather, but with S.E. winds a heavy swell rolls in making the place untenable.

Approach and Anchorage. Approach can be made only by day using the southern entrance. The southern part of the inlet affords the best anchorage, but the bottom being soft mud the holding is unsure. Close by the western shore are three submerged wrecks, one of which is the 18-gun frigate, HMS *Colombine*, sunk in 1834, another is an Austrian brig; but none of them foul the anchorage. At the head of the inlet is a few yards of beach where the lighthouse-keepers (the only inhabitants) haul up their boat in calm weather.

The rightful ownership of this insignificant, deserted island was contested by the British Government in the middle of the last century on the grounds that it was a former Venetian possession and therefore should have been surrendered to Britain. A British squadron was sent to Athens, and the threatened use of forceful measures was only averted by the intervention of that distinguished traveller and Hellenophile, Colonel Leake. The claim was finally dropped.

Proceeding eastwards and passing beyond the deserted Venetico Island you come to the wide **Gulf of Kalamata** or **Messinia.** To the north-east and round the next headland is the other 'Eye of the Republic'—Koroni—an elevated, walled city overlooking the small village with a reasonably sheltered anchorage behind a mole.

Koroni

Approach and Berth. Chart 719 with recent plan of the anchorage elucidates the approach quite clearly by day or night. The fortress walls and bastions are visible a great distance off. 100 yards off the southern shore and up to 70 yards from the breakwater the bottom is short weed and sand. Further out, and west of the extremity of the mole there are some rock slabs.

The anchorage is slightly exposed to the afternoon day breeze from north-west, which may make boat landing rather a wet undertaking.

In the event of sudden N.E. winds a yacht may find anchorage under the lee of Livadia Point.

Port Facilities. These are few, there being only one or two shops for provisions and a good taverna on the water-front.

The Venetian fortress, standing on the hill overlooking the village and port, is interesting to explore. The convent, occupying part of the summit, is inhabited by a number of nuns, who take a great interest in maintaining a colourful flower garden.

An interesting excursion passing through beautiful country is a 20-minute drive to Petriades village. Here is the only place in Greece where in the summer months the large 'Ali Baba' jars (*amphorae*) are made without a wheel—a unique process practised apparently only by this one family in the village.

Continuing on past Koroni to the head of the Messinian Gulf you come to the relatively large commerical port of Kalamata—a very busy place in the autumn months when nearly 300 steamers call to carry away the figs and currants. En route one passes

Petalidhi. Chart 719 (plan). A convenient anchorage off a hamlet, open to winds between north and east, but useful as a sheltered anchorage in event of southerly winds which seldom blow home.

Approach. The low-lying Cape of Petalidhi may be recognized by a white church. One should beware of some rocks and the remains of an ancient mole which extend for 300 yards N.E. of the extremity of the cape.

Anchorage is under the lee of the mole in 2 to 3-fathom depths.

Kalamata (Kalamon) is a commercial port of considerable activity in the autumn months when many steamers call to load with currants.

Approach and Berth. Chart 719. The town is easily distinguished against the hinterland by day, and at night the harbour lights can be seen at only half the distance claimed.

After entering the port, a yacht should make for the north-west corner and berth in the basin with stern to the quay near the Port Office. Mud bottom, and depths of 28 feet nearly everywhere—good shelter.

Officials. As for a Port of Entry.

Facilities. Fresh water, which is good, is laid on to the quay. Fuel is available close by.

A bus runs to Athens three times a day taking 10 hours. A fast train takes about the same time. There is an air service to Athens.

The town of 50,000 people is a quarter of an hour distant, with good shops, an excellent market, and a small modern hotel. A frequent bus service runs from the port. Forty minutes inland by car one reaches a lengthy section of the third-century B.C. walls of Messene which, despite earthquakes, these massive pieces of stone, neatly pieced together, mostly retain their perfect bonding today.

Near the town is the ruined castle of Villehardouin, named after the Crusader Knight, whose heroism and chivalry (revealed in his chronicle) had the effect of stimulating the literary development during the twelfth and thirteenth centuries and sending knights-errant to establish principalities and kingdoms throughout Europe and the Near East.

THE MANI

On the eastern shores of the Messinian Gulf is the rugged and largely barren coast of the high Mani Peninsula. Its mountain ranges ascend to nearly 8,000

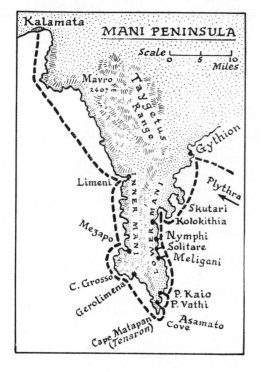

feet and exert a dominating influence on the winds inside these two gulfs. At the southern tip of the peninsula is the insignificant Cape Matapan (Ténaron to the Greeks). The eastern shores are inhospitable, and though **Limeni** is claimed to be a reasonably safe port, it is impossible to lie there comfortably in fresh westerly winds.

From Limeni southwards a number of unusual villages with prominent square towers can be seen from seaward on the hill slopes. This is the country of the Deep Mani, and these Nyklian★ towers were feudal strongholds built from about 1600 onwards by the descendants of the former Nyklian families who came to the under-populated Mani country on the destruction of their own city. Some of these towers are still lived, in, though in other places the villages are largely deserted. They appear more interesting than attractive.

The people nowadays are pleasant enough, but Captain Beaufort, writing 150 years ago, remarked: 'In the district of Maina, the southern province of the Morea, there is a regularly organized system of absolute and general piracy. The number of their vessels or armed row-boats fluctuates between twenty and thirty; they lurk behind the headlands and innumerable rocks of the archipelago; all flags are equally their prey, and the life or death of the captured crew is merely a matter of convenience.'

Southward of Limeni is a small place, **Mezapo,** lying in an open bay with a largely deserted village; and after rounding Cape Grosso with its impressive steep-to cliffs, there is **Gerolimena** with a quay and a few houses, where the steamer calls once a week. At the southern tip of the Mani Peninsula is the uninspiring and low-lying Cape Matapan (Ténaron or Tainaron) with its

★ Described by Patrick Leigh Fermor in *Mani* (John Murray).

'Entrance to the Underworld'. This is the most southerly point of mainland Greece and very nearly the most southerly cape of Europe but Cape Tarifa at the entrance to the Gibraltar Strait wins by 14 miles.

Apart from a call at Koroni a visit by a sailing yacht into this gulf is hardly justified.

Rounding Cape Matapan and entering the **Gulf of Lakonia,** there are some attractive places on the mountainous steep-to Mani shores, but apart from one or two coves shewn in the plans on Chart 712 there are hardly any safe places to leave a sailing yacht for more than an hour or two. This is largely on account of the squalls which may at any time descend with violence from the steep Mani ranges above.

Following on along the **Western Shores** are:

Asamato Cove, comfortable in settled weather when a yacht should anchor in the north-west corner of the bay with a warp to the shore. The bottom here is inconveniently deep and shelves quickly. There is only a fisherman's hut at the head of the creek. This cove is less subject to squalls than some of the other places.

Vathi, known as Port Vathi, is a deep-cut inlet often claimed to be better than Asamato though subject to violent squalls in westerly winds.

Port Kaio. Chart 712 (plan). This is the best shelter near Matapan. Open to north-east, it is possible during adverse conditions to shelter in the northern creek close under the monastery. Usually a yacht anchors in the southern creek in 4 to 5 fathoms on a sandy bottom where holding is good and there is room to swing. One can, however, anchor closer inshore in $2\frac{1}{2}$ fathoms where a short quay and a still shorter 'mole' have been built (5-feet depth at its head). This can be used for the yacht's sternfast and can also provide shelter when landing by dinghy.

The 'towered' village is half an hour's walk up the hill, but hardly worth the effort, for most of the houses are deserted and only thirty people live there. The monastery standing on the hill on the north side of the bay is no longer inhabited. One can walk to the lighthouse on Cape Matapan in an hour, following a goat track passing through the low scrub, which covers most of the hillside, and down to the cave of Ténaron, the entrance to Hades.

The Entrance to the Underworld. In recent years during calm weather a few enterprising Hellenophiles have called here in yachts and caiques to make an examination of this legendary 'Entrance to the Underworld'. One learns that in earlier times Psyche was sent here by Aphrodite to fetch the mysterious casket which was to restore her beauty. Also the bereaved Orpheus when journeying in search of Euridice found his progress blocked by the evil three-headed watch-dog Cerberus, then guarding the cave. To overcome this obstruction Orpheus decided to rely upon his skill with the lute, and very soon Cerberus was lulled to sleep.

Modern explorers while swimming in the semi-darkness of this smooth-sided cave have reported the entire absence of any feeling of mystery. After an underwater examination into the furthest recess they found no sign of any further cave nor any sealed opening. The only inhabitants today are the bats and swallows.

Continuing into Kolokithia Bay, which, though delightful with its green slopes and attractive valleys, provides very few places where one would care to anchor for more than an hour or two in a sailing yacht unless the weather was very settled. These are

> **Meligani,** a small bay, with a few houses, open to the east.
>
> **Solitare,** similar to the above, but more used by small caiques.
>
> **Nymphi,** a narrow rocky inlet 150 yards long with an open beach, and open only to the east.
>
> **Kotronas** lies in a most delightful setting in a small bay with a quay (6 feet); anchorage is in 5 fathoms, close in there are stones on the bottom. Ashore there are a few houses and a taverna, a few fishing boats use the place. As this anchorage is so susceptible to the violent gusts from the hills, a small quay has been built into the rocks about 400 yards southward where caiques usually anchor for better shelter.
>
> **Skutari Bay** (Chart 712) has lovely scenery, but the anchorage is too deep for a yacht—it is liable to strong mountain gusts. In settled weather a yacht can anchor in one of the two coves on the east side of the bay.

Gythion also called **Yithion** (plan on Chart 712) is a pleasant deserted old port with a decaying small town—useful for making excursions to Sparta and Mistra.

> **Approach and Berth.** There are no difficulties day or night, and a yacht should make for the inner harbour. Secure stern to the mole with anchor to the westward in depths of 2 fathoms—bottom is firm clay. Though the harbour appears to be reasonably sheltered, it can in fact be dangerous for a vessel to lie here during strong north-west winds on account of the violent gusts from the Taygetos Mountains. Easterly winds bring in a swell.
>
> **Port Facilities.** Fresh water of poor quality is available by hydrant from the quay which has been extended, with 20-feet depths at its outer end and 17 feet at the inner. Diesel fuel is also obtainable from the quay and petrol from Shell on the quay side. There are ample provision shops with fruit and vegetables; two or three old-fashioned hotels and two restaurants. The

Piraeus steamer calls twice a week; there is a daily bus to Athens (9 hours) and two or three buses a day to Sparta.

The population of Gythion, about 6,000, is still declining since there is little employment here and in the neighbourhood. Many Greek tourists come here for the bathing in the summer months.

The sea walls of the ancient port may be seen under water close off the outflow of the stream north of the town.

A newly constructed road, passing N.W. over the mountains and through attractive, green, cultivated country, enables buses to reach Sparta in an hour. This is a modern town of little concern; but **Mistra,** 15 minutes further has most interesting remains of a Byzantine town standing on a hill overlooking magnificent green country under the Taygetus ranges; several of its churches and convents are still in good order, and the place is well worth a visit.

Elaia, (map p. 61) a very small port with a short mole on its eastern side lies at the foot of a prominent village.

Xyli Bay (also Xili) with the port of **Plythra** is shown on Chart 712. Protected by a long breakwater, it is a dreary barren little place.

Plythra

Approach and berth. The depth off the breakwater in the approach channel is 12 feet and the bottom uneven rocks. By night a hand lantern is exhibited on the molehead. Berth not more than 30 yards inside the molehead with stern to quay, bows northward. Bottom is broken rock, boulders and gravel. Above and below water rocks lie only 60 yards north of the mole. It is not a safe harbour.

Facilities. Very limited provisions to be bought at the hamlet. No good fresh water available. There is a Government Pavilion for a few tourists in summer. Buses run daily to Sparta.

The port was constructed for a shipment of figs from the hinterland and is used in the autumn months. The ancient town lies submerged near the root of the mole.

Elafonisos (Deer) Island, only 12 miles further south, has its village on the eastern end of the boat channel. The hills rise to 900 feet, but are mostly barren. A fine lagoon is formed on the island's western side by a low line of rocks with Elli Islet sheltering the anchorage for a small yacht from all except strong north and westerly winds; but there is nothing of interest ashore.

Vatica Bay, Chart 712, throughout history has provided shelter for the warships of every nation endeavouring to control the western approaches to the

Aegean; there were once Roman and Venetian galleys here and British and German patrol vessels in each World War. Except for providing an excellent lee close under its shores, especially in **Vrakhonisos Petri** (N.W. corner), this large bay is not recommended for a yacht under normal conditions.

Neapolis, a large village on the north-eastern corner of Vatica Bay sometimes a calling place for the steamer, affords little shelter for a yacht.

South of Elafonisos Island is the 4½-mile wide **Elafonisos Channel** separating it from Kithera Island. This channel provides the main route for vessels entering (or leaving) the Aegean from the westward.

Cape Malea, the bold, mountainous headland rising to nearly 2,000 feet, forms the turning point into the Aegean. Since Homeric days this proverbial cape of storms has terrified sailors. The ships of Menelaus narrowly escaped disaster, and one reads of Odysseus being driven southward to the 'Land of the Lotus Eaters'.

For the Ancient Greek sailors making a long voyage perhaps to some distant colony, this noble cape was the last they were to see of their own country for many months to come. 'Round Malea; forget your native country' was the saying attributed to them. Many centuries later, shortly after the heyday of Venice, from the sixteenth until the nineteenth centuries, trading vessels from the West, largely French and British, used to make voyages to the Aegean and Levant.

On a settled day it is interesting to stand close inshore to examine the steep slopes of this rugged cape. The lighthouse keeper may appear on the balcony to acknowledge the hail of a yacht. Close westward is a white hovel—perhaps once a small shrine—where until the Second World War there lived a hermit. In response to a passing ship's siren he would emerge and then raising his arms bestow a blessing as the ship sped past. He is no more, but nearby and standing little more than 100 feet above the sea is a small white monastery. In 1966 there were five nuns here who at the sound of a fog-horn from seaward paraded on the terrace, their black dresses and shawls in telling contrast against the white walls, as they enthusiastically waved their salutations to the passing craft.

One sees very little steamer traffic in these straits today, and as far as the British flag is concerned the present flow of shipping is far less than in the latter half of the last century when trade was flourishing both with Smyrna and the Black Sea ports.

The waters off this cape and also south of Crete were of interest to British vessels in the days of the Levant Company.

The old sailing ships of the seventeenth and eighteenth centuries found the Aegean the height of frustration—as far as Cape Malea relatively good winds had generally filled their sails during the 3,000-mile voyage from England. Now they often found either calms or unfavourable winds and weather. Hardly larger than the Roman corn-ships fifteen centuries earlier, they would round Cape Malea five or six weeks out from Falmouth and then take another two weeks to reach Constantinople only 400 miles further. These voyages persisted until after the Napoleonic Wars.

The Venetian *galleas* squadrons under naval escort also passed under sail through these waters bound for the Levant or Alexandria. They were three-masted vessels of more than 200 feet overall, with a beam ratio of one to four.

The more fortunate vessels found themselves routed to the Levant; often to Iskenderun (Alexandretta) or to Beirut and passing southward to Cape Malea and Crete they sometimes got better winds. An examination of some of these vessels' logs shews that it is not practical to analyse average speeds for passages to the Levant; whereas many ships appear to have made good no more than 2 or at the most 3 knots, there were also a few fast passages. One of these, late in the eighteenth century, was achieved by Nelson's fleet in pursuit of the French towards Egypt. Leaving Messina before a strong westerly wind they passed south of Crete and made good 9 knots in one day and averaged 8—this was, of course, exceptional, also these ships were appreciably larger than the average trader.

On the whole it was little advance on performances by the Roman ships which, often hugging the coast and sailing independently, could reach Egypt from Rome within 20 days—a speed of over 2 knots, although sailing in convoy they made good only $1\frac{3}{4}$ knots. The return voyage was appreciably longer.

THE ISLANDS OF KITHERA AND ANTI-KITHERA WITH THE WESTERN APPROACHES TO THE AEGEAN

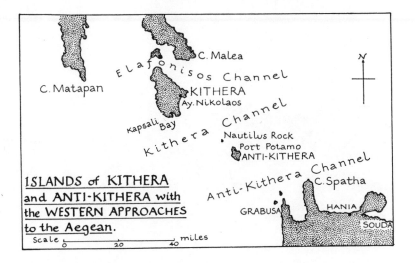

The Western Approaches

ISLAND OF KITHERA

Kapsali Bay
Ayios Nikolaos (Avlemona)
The anchorages of Panaghia and Makri

ISLAND OF ANTI–KITHERA

Port Potamo
Nautilus Rock

4

The Islands of Kithera and Anti-Kithera with the Western Approaches to the Aegean

Weather. Vessels approaching the Aegean usually pass through the 5-mile wide Elafonisos Channel between Cape Malea and Kithera, although the other two channels, each 10 miles in navigable width, are also used by shipping.

The weather in the area of these straits can change quickly, especially in the spring and autumn when the wind may freshen to a strong blow from an unexpected direction. This occurs usually when a depression happens to be passing through the Mediterranean and the wind may spring up suddenly from the eastern quadrant.

Normally in the summer months a westerly wind of moderate strength may be expected, although on reaching Cape Malea it may change and blow freshly from the north according to the strength of the Meltemi at the time. Under these conditions, if shelter is wanted, both the small ports of Kithera are suitable for a yacht, or, in emergency, Grabusa on the west coast of Crete.

Choice of Routes. Having reached the Western Approaches a yacht making for Rhodes must decide whether to pass north of Crete, as the vast majority of yachts do, or sail under the rather blustery and less sheltered south coast.

If deciding to pass northabout, one may follow a description of that coast in *The Aegean: A Sea-Guide*, in which the north coast is described.

The Western Approaches to the Aegean consist of three channels:
Elafonisos, between Elafonisos Island and Kithera. It is nearly 5 miles wide and is used by most vessels approaching the Aegean.

Kithera, between Kithera Island and the groups of unmarked rocks N.W. of Anti-Kithera.

Anti-Kithera, between Anti-Kithera Island and the N.W. promontories of Crete.

> *Forsaken isle! around thy barren shore*
> *Wild tempests howl and wintry surges roar.*
> WALTER RODWELL WRIGHT, *Horar Ionicae* (1807)

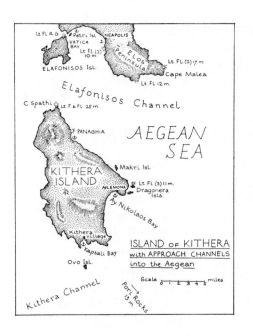

The Island of Kithera is mountainous and steep-to with a barren-looking coast. It has two harbours: on the S.E. coast is Ayios Nikolaos (Avlemona), and there is Kapsali Bay in the south. Also two places of partial shelter on the N.E. coast, suitable for landing under favourable conditions: Panaghia (or Pelayia) with its 100-yard mole, and the sandy lagoon at Makri, but neither is recommended for a yacht.

Kapsali Bay, shown in a plan on Chart 712, lies in a mountainous setting with an anchorage open to the south. It is dominated by a massive Venetian castle. The *chora*, capital of the island, lies 600 feet up and is one of the most attractive little towns in Greece. (See photograph facing page 61.)

Approach and Berth. Chart 712. Lying 2 miles south of the entrance is the conspicuous Ovo Islet, an egg-shaped rock standing at 650 feet. A yacht can either anchor in the bay in 4 fathoms or berth (with caution) behind the rocky spur on which the lighthouse stands, and where shelter is better. The new quay has a depth of only 8 feet, and is useful for securing a sternfast when the yacht has laid out an anchor to the westward. The sea bottom at the anchorage is sand, but near the quay among patches of sand are loose rock and stones, giving uncertain holding. The bay is susceptible to a swell, and untenable in Sirocco winds. In the summer months westerly winds predominate, although northerly weather is frequent.

Facilities. Fresh water, which is good, is available from a tap nearby, and has been piped to the quay; this has been improved and now fuel oil can be provided. Limited provisions can be bought and there is an attractive market at the *chora*.

The *chora*, a full half-hour's climb lies on the hillside in a commanding position beyond the Venetian castle. It was the strength of the castle which so impressed travellers of the sixteenth and seventeenth centuries. Its one gate of entry was always guarded by twenty Italian soldiers and no one might enter without laying down their weapons outside. Six hundred people live in this little island capital; its winding, fascinating streets, with a modest hotel and restaurant and well-stocked shops, are remarkably clean and neat. Good fish and lobsters are often obtainable both here and in the port. People are everywhere friendly and tourists infrequent except in the height of summer. The country, although of no particular attraction, has motor roads to the other villages in the centre of the island.

A palatable Retsina wine—for which the island was once famous—is still exported from Kapsali. The Piraeus steamer calls twice a week. For many years there has been a meteorological station here and one may obtain a useful forecast.

Ayios Nikolaos (Chart 712) is the name of the harbour for the village of Avlemona. The local Greeks also call the harbour Avlemona. Though too small for a large yacht, it is the best harbour in the island, and except in strong southerly winds, when a swell comes in, it is well sheltered.

Berth. A small quay with depths of 3 fathoms is sometimes occupied by caiques, otherwise it is the most suitable place for securing a yacht's sternfast, with her anchor laid out to the southward. The basins are small, but there is swinging room in the outer basin in depths of 3 or 4 fathoms.

Although the configuration of the port is attractive, the barrenness of the surrounding country and the poor decaying hamlet of little white houses makes only a limited appeal to a visiting yacht.

History. When Nelson was Commander-in-Chief the brig *Mentor* carrying seventeen cases containing the famous Elgin Marbles foundered during a gale off the harbour approaches. It was two years before this valuable treasure could be recovered and conveyed to England.

The island has no remarkable history, and like many other Greek islands Kithera has had its share of conquerors. It was colonized first by the Phoenicians who introduced the worship of Aphrodite. The remains of her temple were seen as late as 1551 by the French Court Chamberlain and geographer, Nicholas Daulphinois, when his galley was delayed at Kithera by bad weather. He spent a whole week exploring the island, and describes the ruins of Aphrodite's temple 'on a high mountain'; there were two Ionic columns with others 'four-square' among which was a great portal with 'a statue of a woman clothed in Greek fashion of monstrous size'; the head had been removed and taken to Venice. Below the temple were the remains of the alleged castle of Menelaus, and on Mount St Nicholas were 'two chapels with mosaic pavements showing figures of mounted hunters, harts, lions, bears, dogs and diverse birds'. Today the Sanctuary of Aphrodite has survived in the form of the magnificent fourteenth-century church of Hagios Kosmas.

At this time the island was 'full of woods' and the population very small. It abounded in wild asses having in their heads 'a stone of great virtue'; it was used against 'falling sickness, pain in the flanks, and was laid upon a woman that cannot be delivered of child'.

The most important conquerors were the Venetians, some of whose architecture survives. They regarded Kithera as a watch-post for the gateway to the Aegean, and administered it as part of the Ionian Islands, and so did the British during the period of the Septinsular Republic at the end of the Napoleonic Wars in 1815. It was then garrisoned by a small detachment under a subaltern's command, the garrison being relieved every six months, as it was considered to be 'a very lonely station'. Some English cannon, a bridge and a few graves are the only remains of this British occupation. When restored to Greece in 1864, although still one of the 'Seven Islands', it became administered directly from Athens

Kithera's small population still grows enough to maintain itself, but many migrate to Australia or go to sea.

Between Kithera and Crete is the small island of Anti-Kithera. The 10-mile-wide navigable channels on either side of it are used by vessels proceeding in the direction of Crete.

The Island of Anti-Kithera has a rocky inlet with a hamlet on the north coast, supporting a very small population.

Port Potamo. Chart 712 (plan). It is seldom visited, largely because of the heavy swell which comes in during the prevailing fresh northerly winds.

The only time that Port Potamo came into the news was in the spring of 1900 when a Symi sponge-boat put in to shelter in a small cove S.S.E. of the port. To while away the time at their enforced anchorage, a diver descended to examine the bottom for sponges. He was astonished to find not sponges but statuary. This proved to be original Greek and Roman copies of figures lying on the wreck of an ancient ship which had been conveying them from Greece to Rome. Subsequently, a number were recovered and are now proudly displayed in Athens' museum. The wreck was of a vessel of about 300 tons probably built during the first or second century B.C., and was copper fastened and lead sheathed.

Nautilus Rock—about 10 feet tall—lying about 5 miles N.W. of Anti-Kithera and 2¼ miles S.W. of the conspicuous Pori Islet (410 feet). It is one of a group of rocky islets shown clearly on Chart 1685. This rock is named after the frigate H.M.S. *Nautilus*, wrecked here during the dark hours on the early morning of 3rd January 1807, when homeward bound with urgent dispatches from C.-in-C. to Admiralty. Running southward down the Aegean before a strong northerly wind she had, in the darkness, mistaken the silhouette of the islets for part of Anti-Kithera Island. She altered course to the west and so ran hard up upon the rocks. She soon began to break up, and those of the crew who were able managed to get washed up on the bare rocks where, for five days during the gale without clothing, food or water, they suffered great privation and many perished. On the sixth day four fishing boats came out from Port Potamo and rescued 64 survivors of the total crew of 122.

> *O God have mercy in this dreadful hour*
> *On the poor mariner! In comfort here*
> *Safe sheltered as I am, I almost fear*
> *The blast that rages with resistless power.*
> SOUTHEY, *A Silent Prayer.*

At the subsequent court-martial it was revealed that the rock which *Nautilus* had struck was not marked on the chart.

On the north-west Coast of Crete is the inhospitable anchorage of Grabusa. The nearest safe port is Souda Bay, although in fine weather it is safe to make for Hania, the nearer of the two.

SOUTHERN CRETE

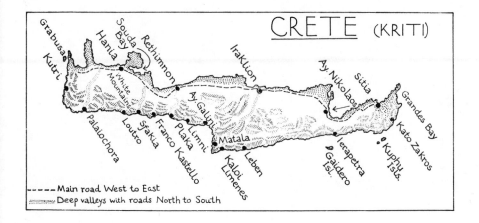

----- Main road West to East
▦▦▦ Deep valleys with roads North to South

GENERAL INFORMATION

West Coast
  Grabusa (Grambousa)
  Kutri

South Coast
  Palaiochora
  Loutro Bay
  Sfakia
  Gavdo Island
  Franco Kastello
  Plaka Bay
  Limni
  Ayia Galini (Erimoupolis)
  Matala
  Kaloi Limenes (Fair Havens)
  Leben
  Ierapetra
  Gaidero Island
  Kuphu Islands

East Coast
  Kato Zakros
  Grandes Bay
  Palaiokastro
  Kouremenos
  Erimoupolis
  Dhaskalia Bay
  Ayios Ioannes

5
Southern Crete

Odysseus sailing in a Phoenician ship to Libya passed
under the lee of Crete, but 'when we had put Crete
astern the hostile Zeus brought on a storm'.

The Odyssey

This large island, known as Kriti to the Greeks, was once the centre of the Western World. With a length of about 140 miles, it is Greece's longest and tallest island with a chain of mountains rising to more than 8,000 feet.

More than half the island is barren; on the northern slopes are elevated plains with rich cultivation. Here are most of the villages and towns which accommodate the bulk of the half-million inhabitants.

On the southern shore the scenery is wild and grand, remarkable for the steep mountain terrain and the deep narrow ravines which, cutting through the mountains, form arteries of communication between the south and the more important towns in the north. There are no forests surviving today, but there are still extensive chestnut woods at the western end, and the high mountains are lightly sprinkled with cypresses,* firs and a few cedars. In the deep valleys are sometimes to be found masses of oleanders.

Those expecting to find this mountainous coast refreshingly green will be disappointed; but in the great valleys, cutting through the ranges, no finer or more diverse scenery could be found anywhere. There are a large number of olives and carob trees; often a rich red soil growing every kind of market-garden produce, and winding villages of little white houses avenued with mulberry and eucalyptus.

The rivers which once flowed continuously to the coast have mostly become torrents and run only after the winter rains, because the forests were felled for the African timber trade in Minoan days and later, and the rainfall has declined. This is not the only change during the last three thousand years, for significant corrugations have appeared on the southern shores causing considerable changes

* According to Pliny this island was the original home of the cypress, and in Hellenic days they could be seen among the snowfields of the White Mountains.

in the character of the coast. Parts of the east coast have risen at least 20 feet while on the south the shore has subsided some 15 feet. One may see today a former Minoan port raised high above the cliffs and elsewhere cave dwellings now deep under water.

From seaward one may sometimes see small villages standing on a hilly ledge surrounded by a small patch of cultivation. Beneath them on the coast were the small Minoan ports, some of which were revived by the Venetians and still survive today though they are mostly no longer of significance except for sheltering small local craft. A few terraces can also be seen climbing from the valleys up the mountain slopes, but their cultivation has been neglected for centuries. In the higher terrain are only sheep and goats.

Those who took part in the Battle of Crete will have nostalgic memories of these shores. It may be remembered that early in 1941 the ships of the Royal Navy had been severely damaged by the Luftwaffe, and bombed out of the Aegean. It was then realized that no longer having naval support the garrison of 32,000 must be evacuated from Crete. After suffering much damage and many casualties the Navy set forth once more from Alexandria for their final task with the Army. 'They started the evacuation overtired' wrote Lord Cunningham, '. . . and had to carry it through under savage air attack . . . it is perhaps even now not realized how nearly the breaking point was reached. But that these men struggled through is a measure of their achievement'. Making use of the beaches at Erimoupolis (Ayia Galini, where there is now a small port), Sfakia, and the beaches at Grandes Bay they rescued half the garrison, others being brought off from Iraklion. Though the best part of the troops were saved, the Navy lost heavily both in ships and men: two cruisers and two destroyers being sunk close southward of Crete as well as several others in the vicinity. These small Minoan ports, though mostly occupied by the Germans for the next three years, were used continuously for landing liaison officers and stores to sustain the Cretan Resistance until the end of the war.

Food and Drink. The type of food in Crete is no different from the rest of Greece but the standard for tourists is lower. Fish is sometimes rather less plentiful, but fruit and vegetables probably in better supply: oranges, bananas and figs are excellent. On the south coast provisions generally are limited and the standard of comfort is appreciably lower than elsewhere.

Wine. Red: try Brousko and Kissamos. White: Minos and Gortys, although there are several other kinds according to taste. The local draught wine is often good. There is also local vermouth and brandy, both quite palatable of their kind. No Retsina wine is made anywhere in Crete. Athens 'Fix' beer is also available and two other local brews.

The Cretans, a very independent people, are similar in many ways to the Greeks, although anthropologists point out certain features of the Venetians and Turks, their masters for many centuries. The Venetians were driven out by the Turks in the 17th century, losing their last stronghold, Candia, after a 20-year siege, in 1669. After this Crete remained Turkish for 250 years reverting to Greece only at the beginning of the twentieth century.

The local country costume is unmistakably Turkish in character. If one travels by bus to the outlying villages, a number of peasant landowners attired in Cretan dress may still be seen: long, black boots reaching to the knee, black breeches with a huge bag behind (a relic of the tradition that Mohammed is to be born of man), a red or blue cummerbund, and above this a waistcoat that proclaims the character of the wearer. The waistcoat is made of different materials and colours and in many styles, usually cut fairly high and with rakishly set buttons which might well rival the mess kits of our smartest regiments. Often a white silk shirt with sleeves is worn, but no tie; and around the head is an Arab type of *agal* in blue, red or black. One often sees men in this costume, in a cafe veranda sitting with great dignity watching others while away the time at cards and tric-trac; they themselves seem aloof from such dissipation. All the young men, and the women, too, now wear ordinary western clothes, and in less than a generation the traditional costume will have vanished.

Before describing the south coast ports, it is necessary first to give brief details of the west coast anchorages.

Grabusa or **Grambousa.** A deserted anchorage in a dramatic setting by an off-lying island among steep cliffs.

> **Approach** (Chart 1631) may be made either east or south of Grabusa Island, recognized by the Venetian fortress standing at 450 feet on the western cliffs.
> **Anchorage** is on the south side of Grabusa. The place is not safe in strong winds from the S.W., but it is, however, excellent shelter in northerly gales, and a number of small Greek vessels make good use of it today.
> **Facilities.** There are none. Only a couple of shepherds are sometimes there to look after the sheep and goats brought round by caique from Kastelli on the north coast.

Although the island is deserted today the anchorage is often used by local craft waiting for north winds to moderate.

The supporting walls and some of the gateways into the Venetian fortress are still in good preservation. There is no means of access from the opposite shore on the mainland of Crete.

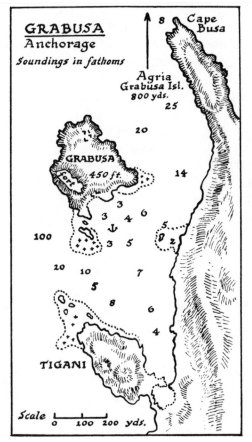

GRABUSA
Anchorage
Soundings in fathoms

History. At the time of the Greek War of Independence this place was a thorn in the flesh to the shipping of all countries entering the Aegean. In the two years before 1827 (when piracy was partly subdued) no less than 155 vessels were pirated and their cargoes brought in here for sale. Of these vessels, 28 were under the British flag. To protect shipping nine sloops of the British Navy were allocated to the archipelago, and in 1828 an Anglo-French expedition was organized to destroy the base at Grabusa.* In February of the following year, while attempting to beat into the anchorage in pursuit of some pirates, H.M. brig *Cambria*, due to an accident, missed stays and was wrecked on the reef south of the islet.

When Grabusa was captured, 6,000 people were found on the island with 3,000 muskets and captives both male and female—'Such misery and wretchedness I never beheld,' wrote the Senior Naval Officer, 'many hundreds of them living in holes in the rocks.' The expedition destroyed all the pirate boats and found a certain amount of plundered property which was put on board the transport *Ann and Amelia* for conveyance to Malta. After this expedition there were only minor acts of piracy in the Aegean; these did not cease until the middle of the last century.

The Changing Coastline. Following the coast southwards for 6 miles you come to the headland of **Kutri.** The few ruins now remaining are those of the ancient city of Phalasarna described by Strabo as possessing an artificial port and a temple sacred to Artemis. Captain Spratt, a surveyor, making some careful studies of Crete in the middle of the last century, has proved that the coastline of S.W. Crete has risen considerably since the days of Greek and Roman geographers; in some places the shore, together with its ancient ports, lies as much as 26 feet above the present sea level. The greatest upheaval was further

* This was probably the first organized expedition to stamp out piracy since that of Pompey eighteen centuries earlier. On that occasion he captured 846 vessels and took many captives, largely from the small Cilician ports.

Methoni: the walls of Modon

Crete: Grabusa, the solitary anchorage

The Island of Karpathos: Port Pigadhia

Crete: Sitia, a temporary anchorage on the north-east coast

east between Selino and Lissus (Agios Kirkos) where certain ports, once the sea outlets for some Hellenic mountain towns, have entirely disappeared.

Phalasarna harbour resembles a Roman galley port, being hewn from the solid rock, *it now lies 20 feet up above the cliffs*. Since the sketch below, taken

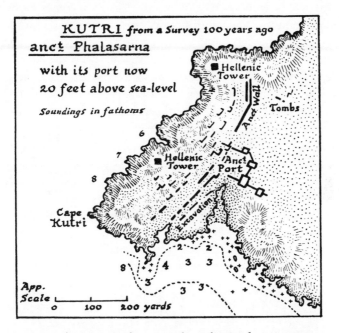

from Captain Spratt's survey, the coast has changed again. Now, a hundred years later, a recent examination of the coast by the Greek surveyors shows that considerable deposits of sand have filled in the small inlets and brought the fathom contours more than 100 yards away from the land.

This place is not an anchorage for a yacht, although in calm weather one may anchor temporarily in 3 fathoms and land by a rough track. Large vessels sometimes anchor under the lee of Petalides Islet half a mile to the S.W.

South Coast

These fierce flaws are beyond my knowledge. From all directions the seas run at us, and amongst the hurly-burly the black ship drives.
ALCAEUS. 600 B.C.

There are no entirely secure harbours on the south coast of Crete, but in the summer it is reasonably safe to make use of anchorages in certain bays. The most troublesome enemy of the sailing yacht is the hard gusts which, with fresh north winds, blow strongly down from the mountains. So hard are these gusts off the S.E. coast that *Sailing Directions* warn sailing vessels to keep 5 miles off. This coast is, therefore, recommended only for yachts with power.

When visiting these ports it is sometimes interesting to bear in mind their earlier importance in Minoan days when they had a lively trade with Africa, and again in Roman times when this trade, especially with Egypt, was revived. When the Venetians came in the thirteenth century, sea trade was again revived though it had shifted mainly to the north coast. Four centuries later, when under Turkish rule, commerce fell to a low ebb and on the south coast, there were only a few Cretan ship-owners with small schooners; the Turks, however, fearing raids by pirates, established a coastguard service, each headland having watch-men who could communicate by a system of fire signals.

With regard to the anchorages described in the following pages only two ports are considered to be undisturbed and safely sheltered: Loutro Bay traditionally considered to be safe all the year round, and the recently construc-ted Ayia Galini. The latter is more suitable and convenient for a yacht.

Temporary anchorage at the western end of the coast can be found at:

Palaiochora, a prominent headland with a small village affording sheltered anchorage either side of its isthmus according to the weather.

Approach and Anchorage. (Plan on Chart 1633). The low walls of the Venetian fortress stand out clearly, and normally a vessel proceeds to the anchorage of the village. There are depths of 2½ fathoms 200 to 300 yards east of a small stone pier. Here the bottom is sandy, but closer inshore are rocks. The bay is completely open between E.N.E. and south, and in strong northerly winds the anchorage on the west side of the promontory is to be preferred.

Towards the S.E. extremity of the peninsula there is a very small and inadequate harbour used by the local fishing craft. According to fishermen there are 2-fathom depths at the entrance and patches of sand between the rocks, on which one may anchor.

Facilities. Limited fresh provisions can be bought. There is a very modest hotel and some eating places. The village has electricity, but there is no ice. A road leading northwards over the mountains passes through a most attractive country and reaches Hania. A bus runs daily, the journey taking 3 hours. A caique sails every Wednesday for Gavdo Island—20 miles—and returns the following day.

The village, with a thousand inhabitants, is attractive, Its main street is avenued with mulberry trees and acacias; the kerb and the sills of the little houses are meticuously washed in white. The people are either employed in an olive oil factory or in fishing. The Venetian fortress has only its poorly-fashioned retaining walls surviving, the rest having been quarried long ago.

Kandano, with its Byzantine churches and frescoes, is some 40 minutes' inland by the bus.

Following the coast eastwards beyond Cape Flomi one comes to the wildest and most picturesque scenery on the coast: passing beneath the White Mountains one reaches Tripiti, where two conspicuous crags meet at the entrance to the Gorge of Samaria—further inland are terraces on the side of a hill with vestiges of early habitation by the village of Ayia Roumeli. In very calm weather one may anchor off Tripiti, but it is normally advisable to go to Loutro.

Loutro Bay (Phoenix of the *Acts*) has traditionally been considered the most sheltered anchorage in southern Crete.

Approach. (Plan on Chart 1633). Coming from the west a small white church stands conspicuously by the point and above it a buff-coloured Turkish watch-tower. There is deep water everywhere.

Anchorage. Anchor in convenient depths with ship's head pointing about E.S.E. and lay out a stern anchor. Both the holding and the shelter are good. In winter Sirocco gales the wind does not blow home, only a swell enters the bay; to guard against this eventuality vessels weight their cable. The anchorage is normally comfortable in a strong wind, although it suffers damage from a whirlwind during winter storms.

Facilities. There are none—only a small taverna. There is no water supply, except that collected in private cisterns; and there is no easy land communication except by rough foottracks to Sfakia and Anapolis.

The hamlet of a dozen small white houses lies at the foot of steep, bare mountains; only one building known as 'The Chancery' stands out. A few tamarisks and a tall palm tree complete this peaceful setting. About seventy people live there, some being young seamen who are often away. Half a dozen small fishing craft provide the means of livelihood.

Local Roman inscriptions have proved that Loutro (anct. Phoenix) was a port frequented by Alexandrian shipping. According to St Luke's description in *Acts* (27.12) it was 'an haven of Crete that lieth towards south-west and north-west'. This would imply that he was describing the bay of Foinikos lying on the west side of the promontory, and not the far better sheltered Loutro Bay on the east side, and facing east. However, some of the local people still refer to the ancient Phoenix as having been situated by the fragmentary remains at Foinikos.

The port, mentioned by Strabo, was the outlet for Anopolis, now only a small inland village on the hillside; but some columns and arches as well as remains show that it was once a place of importance.

The spectacular Gorge of Samaria can be reached via Anopolis to Ayia Roumeli, an exhausting walk often through steep hilly country. Ayia Roumeli village lies at the bottom of the gorge, and from here a rough shaded track ascends for 11 kilometres reaching Xyloskalon with its tourist pavilion. Some distance beyond is the road towards Lakkoi, the terminal for the Hania bus. In settled weather small local boats can be hired at Sfakia to take one to Loutro ($\frac{1}{2}$ hour) and Ayia Roumeli (2 hours).

After the Venetian epoch the place continued to operate a fleet of small square-riggers, fifteen or sixteen of which went on laying-up there until after the period of Napoleon. After this, trade began to decline, and by the middle of the last century the people were known for their 'lawless daring and deeds'. This was probably when the Turks built the small fort on the point and the castle on the hill slope, both of which still survive. Terraces and olive trees are still to be seen on the slopes above the hamlet, but cultivation has obviously been neglected for many decades.

Together with Sfakia, 3 miles eastward, these two little hamlets are as poor and neglected as anywhere in Greece. Recently there seemed a possibility of Loutro regaining its importrance, for an oil company, wishing to provide a base for bunkering west-bound tankers from Syria, carried out a survey. No doubt they were deterred by the impossibility of constructing roads to the

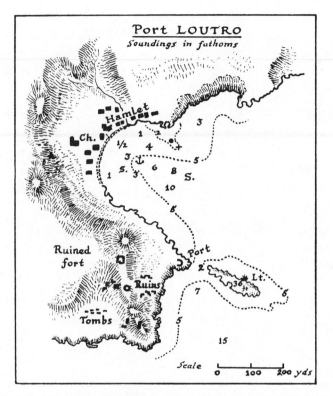

interior through the steep mountains, and so Fair Havens (Kaloi Limenes) was selected instead.

Sfakia is a very small hamlet with convenient anchorage for steamers off the coast; there is little disturbance from the strong north winds, and it is possible to land at a small boat harbour below the hamlet.

There is a daily bus communication with Hania in 6 hours.

Once a village of importance with 3,000 people, it has largely crumbled away; only about 200 inhabitants remain. On 22nd May, 1941, the King of Greece was embarked here in a British cruiser to avoid capture by German forces.

The off-lying island of **Gavdo** (1,140 feet) is the Clauda of St Paul; flat and uninteresting, it lies 20 miles south of Crete. Its few inhabitants are peasants, formerly from Sfakia, but now their ties are with Palaiochora. In the summer months one can land near a cluster of houses on the N.W. coast, a short distance from Kastri. Landing can also be made on the east coast, at a shingle beach with a small pier, which is used by the mail caique from Palaiochora.

97

Apart from 'Calypso's vaulted cavern' and some arched rocks there is nothing to see. When Captain Spratt came here more than a century ago he described the local people, mostly from Sfakia, as being 'a mixed and degenerate race' and expressed surprise when several of them swam out 'boarding his ship in a state of nudity.'

Franco Kastello is an anchorage protected by a cape 6 miles east of Sfakia. A substantial Venetian castle, entirely deserted and roofless, stands by the cape on the edge of an extensive plain, and extending in a S.E. direction 6 cables from the castle is a reef.

Anchorage in 2 or 3 fathoms is in a small bay close northward but with strong north winds there are mountain gusts.

Continuing eastwards one comes to two coves, neither being of interest apart from the scenery:

Plaka Bay, 8 miles east and 1½ miles north of the headland of Kaka Muri, is suitable in settled weather for temporary anchorage.

Limni, a small cove at the mouth of a ravine lies 5 miles east of Plaka. It may be recognized by a monastery on the hill a mile westward; the place was used by the British for minor operations against the Germans between 1941 and 1943.

Ayia Galini (Erimoupolis). The only artificial port on the south of Crete, and in the summer months the most sheltered port of call.

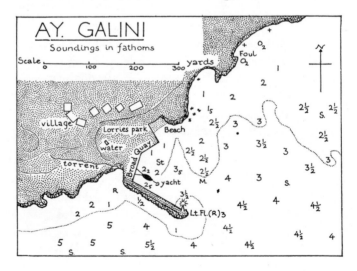

Approach. A tall substantial mole with a quay extends for 150 yards in a direction about 115° from the western side of the hamlet. At its extremity is a short tower with a light, and above the root, about 60 feet high, is an obelisk. The mole, with tall protecting wall, is easily distinguished from seaward. There are depths of 30 feet off the molehead decreasing to 12 feet at its root by a broad quay.

Berth. A yacht should berth either stern to the mole or off the broad quay by its root (12 feet) where there is a fresh-water tap. The port is well sheltered except in southerly winds, and the summer Meltemi causes little concern. The bottom is sand.

Officials. Harbour Master and Customs.

Facilities. Two small inns, modest tavernas, and very limited fresh provisions.

The port was built in 1953 and serves the purpose of shipping to Athens the fresh produce of the Messara Plain which arrives in lorries from Timbaki village and is loaded into small steamers alongside. The hamlet, a poor little place without interest, has a population of about 500, some of whom are employed in an oil-cake factory. A few fishing craft usually go off to Africa in the spring and summer months. Westward of the mole are some remarkable caves set in the vertical cliffs by the water.

A bus runs to Iraklion twice a day—$2\frac{1}{2}$ hours.

The usefulness of Ayia Galini to a yacht is that she can usually be left here in safety while one goes off to visit the Minoan ruins at Phaestos and Ayia Triada. A taxi can be hired from Timbaki.

Messara Bay. The long beach extending southwards nearly to Matala is of no interest from seawards. When viewed from the hinterland at Ayia Triada (the famous Minoan summer palace standing on the hill), the valley leading towards the beach may be seen to open on a beautifully wooded and cultivated plain.

It seems apparent that with the drying up of the river, which many centuries ago flowed out of the great Messara Plain, the same process of nature has repeated itself as in Ionian Anatolia, i.e. the silt from the river no longer being carried swiftly to the sea has gradually been deposited in the river-bed and has built up a large flood plain; the sea and the waves have overcome the small outflow of water at the river-mouth and sealed the river exit with a beach.

In late medieval times there was a last attempt to maintain a port for shipments of produce from this plain: at Kokinos Pyrgos at the northern end of the beach are remains of port buildings, but until the recent opening of a port at Ayia Galini there has been no proper sea export of Messara produce for centuries.

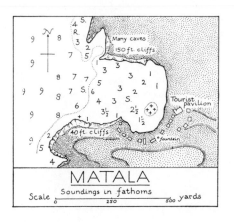

Matala. Chart 2536A (plan). A horse-shoe shaped bay with a good bathing beach—suitable for temporary anchorage.

Approach and Anchorage. The bay may be recognized by the white cliffs on the northern side of the entrance. Anchor anywhere convenient off the sandy beach.

The bay is open to the westerly swell caused by the day breeze, and can attract mountain gusts in the event of strong north winds.

Facilities. The new Tourist Pavilion has limited supplies. There are half a dozen small houses at the back of the sandy beach.

In late Minoan times Matala was the port for Phaestos, and according to *The Odyssey* some of Menelaus's ships were driven ashore here when returning from Troy. Later, in the Roman epoch, there is evidence of the place having been used as an outlet for Gortyna (the provincial capital) for trade with African ports. At that time, Matala was probably a deep, sheltered inlet cut into the gorge. During the centuries the coast has changed: the cliffs have sunk and the inlet has subsequently been closed by the formation of a beach.

Some of the caves are now 10 to 15 feet under water, others still above water are used nowadays by summer campers. The presence of very eroded bollards hewn from the rock in the cliffside suggest that trading vessels have used this place in later centuries; some storage tanks also suggest the later use of this port.

With the building of a Tourist Pavilion and the construction of a new motor road from Phaestos the ancient port of Matala may soon become a small summer resort.

Kaloi Limenes (Fair Havens). A small bay open to the eastward with a few decaying houses and poor road communications.

Approach and Anchorage. See recent plan on Chart 1633. The church of St Paul is conspicuous. Proceed into the bay and anchor in $2\frac{1}{2}$ fathoms 200 yards off the hamlet. There are less gusty winds here than many places and S.E. gales do not blow home.

Facilities. There is practically nothing here except a taverna, the few inhabitants being very poor.

The bay has recently been developed by an oil combine with a view to

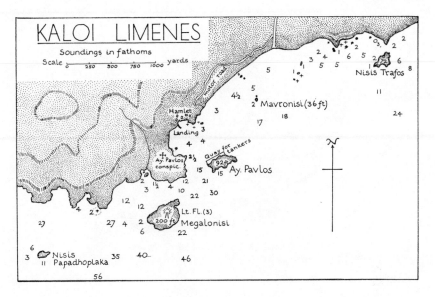

making Kaloi Limenes into a bunkering station for homeward-bound tankers coming from the Levant. The fuel depot-ship formerly moored under the lee of Pavlos Islet has been replaced by a quay on the islet itself. The steep, rough road over the mountains to Iraklion has been improved.

History. In A.D. 59 when St Paul was en route from Myra to Rome in a corn ship, they had been forced by the strong N.W. winds in the Aegean to pass under the S.E. of Crete. They reached Fair Havens. The question of wintering here arose; it was now after 5 October, and not considered safe to continue the voyage so late in the season. It would appear that they had a conference on board where, against Paul's advice, a decision was made to sail for the next port on the coast—Phoenix (almost certainly Loutro Bay) nearly 40 miles further. In *Acts* 27, the narrative continues: 'When a south wind sprang up they imagined that it answered their purpose and setting sail coasted along keeping close in to the shore. But before long a squally off-shore North-easter blew up and hit the ship, which was unable to head into it, so we let ourselves be carried along. We ran under the lee of the little island called Clauda and managed with some difficulty to haul in the ship's boat.'

A fortnight later they were wrecked at Malta. (See plan overleaf.)

St Luke's description of the wind's direction as N.E. does not quite make sense in the narrative that follows. The controversial word is *Euroclydon*, whose exact meaning has been disputed. If N.E. was intended—an unusual wind off this coast—where the deep mountain valleys govern the direction—it would have suited the Roman corn-ship and given her an easy sail to Phoenix. Quite clearly it did not.

Roman Merchant Vessel – about 2nd. century, A.D.
Sketch from a model in the *Science Museum*
(about 250 tons burden)

But having started with a southerly wind—'which answered their purpose'—
it seems likely that after reaching Cape Litinos the wind headed them, coming
in freshly from the north, that is from the Cretan mountains. A change of wind
from this direction—a natural occurrence with a passing depression—would
make nautical sense of the narrative, and explain how the vessel was headed
off from the land by this strong wind, and, 'being unable to head into it', made

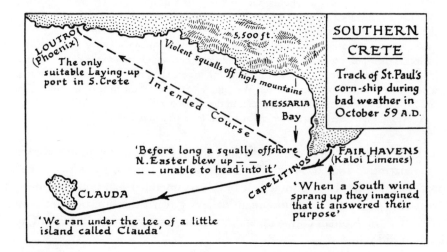

for the lee of Clauda where they 'managed with some difficulty to haul in the ship's boat'.

An accurate record of a repetition of these weather conditions occurred almost exactly eighteen centuries later when the British Admiralty's auxiliary survey vessel *Spitfire* had put to sea from Fair Havens.

On this occasion, in October, 1852, *Spitfire* experienced light flaws of wind from south and sometimes off the land. She accordingly raised steam to obtain some assistance from her paddles. On rounding Cape Litinos the wind suddenly sprang up from the north, soon reaching gale strength. Only by raising a full pressure of steam did *Spitfire* eventually reach the head of Messara Bay and there obtain some shelter under the land while the gale continued.

Southern Crete—The coast looking towards Kaloi Limenes (*after Captain Spratt*)

Leben or **Leda** is a small open cove close under the prominent headland of Kephalo (or Leon), which resembles a crouching lion. It lies 6 miles east of Kaloi Limenes. In 3 fathom depths there is shelter from the west, but the sea can be rather disturbed.

Formerly called Lebina, it was a port for Gortyna at the end of the Minoan period, and was also renowned for its medicinal spring waters which are still collected and bottled for sale in Crete. Some Minoan remains can be seen on the peninsula and a later Greek temple of Asclepius on the hillside—a long climb to get there. Only about fifty people live in the hamlet with three or four small fishing boats which they haul up on the beach.

Ierapetra. An open anchorage off the largest village on the south of Crete. Chart 1633 (Plan).

Approach. The village, standing against a barren background, is easily recognized from seaward. The chimney and minaret are both conspicuous, and the small ruined fort on the headland.

Berth. The anchorage is in the N.W. corner of the bay in convenient depths on a sandy bottom. Open between E. and S. from which quarter a swell often rolls in.

The ancient harbour, largely silted now, has insufficient depth even for small craft. Small fishing boats use the northern side of the short quay to land their catch; but this affords no shelter whatever against the swell, and in S.E. weather local boats are all hauled up.

Facilities. In recent years a modern village has grown up with a small hotel and one or two less pretentious ones. There are two or three good eating places, and prices are low. A local wine, rather sweet, claimed to be a type of sparkling Burgundy, can be bought.

This village, with a population of 9,000, has been of importance throughout the centuries. During the Roman era it was quite a large town with three small harbours. Travellers in medieval times have described the ruined amphitheatre, two theatres, temples, baths and aqueducts. At that time it was a village surrounded by walls, but in 1508 a severe earthquake destroyed everything and today the present village and the small Venetian fortress stand on the site of the original medieval architecture embedded in the walls of some of the modern houses; there is also a mosque, now turned into a concert hall. A small museum of Minoan finds attracts visitors.

Long before Roman times, however, it was of some importance in the middle Minoan period, as a number of recovered terracotta ornaments, vases, and double axe-heads (in copper) can testify. Collections of these may seen in the Ashmolean Museum at Oxford. Two fine Parian marble sarcophagi of a much later period, brought off by H.M.S. *Medina* in 1860, are now in the British Museum together with other ornaments.

A number of Greeks and a few foreign tourists come here in the summer for the good bathing off the sandy beach.

A road leads over the mountains to Ay. Nikolaos and Iraklion with bus communication three or four times daily (4 hours).

Gaidero is an uninhabited island of no interest, but in an emergency can provide anchorage under its lee from southerly gales. Fishing boats from Ierapetra sometimes fish in this area.

EAST COAST

Lying off the S.E. corner of Crete are the **Kuphu Islands**; uninhabited and waterless, they are distinguished by their white cliffs. The largest of the group is low and flat. All are now uninhabited, but both in Roman and medieval times there was a small population. A few ruins of the Roman period remain.

Proceeding north-eastwards for 6 miles one comes to Ampelos, with Kavallos Bay anchorage; but, on account of the violent squalls, during the Meltemi season a yacht is recommended to give this part of the coast a wide berth. Four and a half miles further is the sandy Zakro Bay.

Kato Zakros. Anchor off the hamlet in convenient depths. The hamlet lies at the foot of a ravine with a rough road from Upper Zakros leading eventually to Sitia. Simple provisions can be bought.

The interest in the place is the excavated Minoan site. Although examined by the British archaeologist Hogarth in 1901 when Zakros was then judged to have been an early trading port for Africa, recent excavations have revealed the remains of a large Minoan palace probably of the period about 1,500 B.C. Many vases, storage jars, copper ingots, tools, ivory tusks etc. have been recovered from the ruins and sent to Iraklion Museum, and others have found their way to the Ashmolean Museum in Oxford. This palace is one of the four to be excavated in Crete. Visitors who expect to see its restoration as grand and realistic as that at Knossos could be disappointed; but if they visit the museums of Greece, England, Germany, they will be astonished to see such a high standard in the delicate terracotta pottery and the exquisite ornamental jewellery recovered from these Minoan palaces and sea-ports.

Grandes Bay. On Chart 1677, can be seen detailed plans of anchorages which, under certain conditions are suitable for sheltering a yacht. The bay is entered after rounding the steep-to Cape Plaka which was, with little doubt, the Cape Salmone of the *Acts* where St Paul's ship made her landfall in late September A.D. 59 after leaving Cnidos bound for Rome.

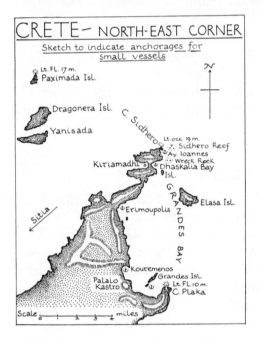

The prevailing wind in the summer months is northerly, though during September the N.W. wind is prominent. Strong winds are usually preceded by haze and humidity.

In the southern part of this large bay, where the shore is often encumbered with rocks, are some small landing places with occasional anchorages where local caiques during summer collect farm produce and convey it to the north coast ports. There is

Palaiokastro, once a Minoan town standing on the hillside close to the shore. The acropolis has been excavated and the few objects recovered have been sent elsewhere. Close south of this hill is a landing place with a rough road leading towards the village which has now become a farming centre. The landing place is very exposed. A pleasant bathing beach lies to the northward—about 2 miles from the village.

The fortified monastery of Toplou is only 5 miles from here and can be reached by a rough road. The monastery formerly had its own guns for defence against pirates. It was founded in the fourteenth century but largely rebuilt in 1718, and has rather a gloomy appearance.

Kouremenos, a mile northwards, has a 2-fathom anchorage off a sandy bay where there is shelter except in easterly weather.

The local craft at both Kouremenos and Palaiokastro, if suddenly overtaken by easterly weather, seek shelter under the lee of the S.W. extremity of the Grandes islet.

Erimoupolis, (Itanos), some 4 miles north of Kouremenos, has good sheltered anchorage close offshore on a sandy bottom at the northern end of the bay. Limited fragmentary remains of the Greek, Roman, and Byzantine periods and part of an early Christian church can be seen close to the shore. Now, the place is utterly deserted, but it was once a sizeable Roman port where freighters sailing from Egypt would put in to shelter and perhaps await favourable weather to help them continue into the Aegean. In about 1850 some inscriptions supporting this history were recovered among the ruins and are now in the Fitzwilliam Museum at Cambridge, but the Ashmolean has the best collection of Minoan pottery in England.

At the base of the next valley south of the ruins is the sandy beach of Vai with its clusters of stunted palm-trees.

Following the coast, with its barren hills, northward and passing inside the uninhabited island of Elasa you come to

Dhaskalia Bay, affording shelter in north and west winds, and often used by local craft.

The coast now continues towards the northern point of this promontory, and after passing two small headlands one reaches

Ayios Ioannes. This is a delightful little creek suitable for a small yacht in peaceful deserted surroundings.

> **Approach.** After leaving Dhaskalia Bay care should be taken to avoid a small group of rocks (mostly under water) lying 400 yards off shore. There is a safe passage inside. These rocks are referred to on the earlier English charts as 'Wreck Rock'.
> **Anchorage.** A yacht should enter the centre of this 2-fathom creek heading in the direction of the lighthouse. Moor head and stern. A ledge with depths of only one fathom extends for about 50 yards from the shore.

There are no inhabitants except the lighthouse-keepers who usually haul up their boat on the beach at the head of the creek.

Rounding Cape Sidhero. The land falls away towards the cape (with its prominent lighthouse). There is a clear passage of 600 yards when passing inside the Sidhero Reef some of whose rocks are awash or showing above water.

On the west coast of the Sidhero promontory is the sheltered inlet of Kiriamadhi Bay and 10 miles further is the port of **Sitia.** (See '*The Aegean': a Sea-Guide.*) This however, is not a safe anchorage in N.E. winds, when a yacht should make for the gulf of Mirabella and berth in the northern creek of Ayios Nikolaos, distant 30 miles from Cape Sidhero.

Sponge Fishing off the east coast of Crete provides some of the best quality sponges. Divers from Kalimnos and Symi, who in the middle of the last century dived here without apparatus, appeared at the turn of the century in helmets, suits and weighted boots; now they are gradually being replaced by skin-divers, whose performance is more efficient. The Turks have a rival sponge industry operating off the Anatolian coast, and the Levant countries also have a few sponge divers. No longer does one see a diver enter the sea with a 20-lb slab of marble held at arms' length to act as a horizontal rudder.

The modern 15-ton motor *trehandiri* some years ago replaced the early sponge fishing boats encountered by British ships in the last century. Then they were smaller, sprit-rigged with long bowsprits, and carrying topsails.

The divers, who work in groups of half a dozen or more, arrive on their station early in May and then prepare for their task. When divers worked without some form of compressed air they could not at first remain in depths

Sponge boats, after a sketch by Captain Spratt (mid-19th century)

of more than 12 to 15 fathoms without suffering from a bleeding nose, and since the best sponges, as Aristotle observed, 'come from the greater depths',

Rhodes: Lindos, showing the harbour with the citadel beyond

Rhodes: the entrance to Mandraki Harbour

they had to accustom themselves to working in 20 to 30 fathoms. Unassisted, a diver could stay down $1\frac{1}{2}$ to 2 minutes, but with compressed air, either in the rubber suit or with Nargile* apparatus, they remain down gathering sponges until their net is filled.

Accidents are rare, and although a diver subconsciously fears attack by sharks it is seldom that one is made. In the days of Pliny it was the dogfish they feared, especially the prospect of attack during their ascent to the surface. It is usually in later life that the ill-effects of deep-diving are felt.

For many generations Greek divers have come largely from the island of Kalimnos and some from Symi, as they do today; formerly a few came also from Rhodes and Tilos. Turkish divers mostly come from Bodrum.

In Roman days the best sponges were brought up from the shores off Cape Malea and Lycia. But today for various reasons the most successful sponge-fishing takes place off the North African coast, although off the shores of Crete, both on the east coast and near Ayia Galini, sponges are still gathered. In the Levant, after the Second World War, sponge-diving has again been taken up; here they are not handicapped by the more conservative methods with rubber-suits, but learn at once the modern free-diving technique. Their sponges, however, with the exception of those found near the island of Ruad, are of inferior quality, and some of these divers go to Cyprus where the industry has not so far been exploited.

Turkish sponge boat, a *trehanderi*, with rubber suit
and ladder being prepared for the diver's descent.

* Compressed air is pumped into a tank; thence a high-pressure hose conveys the air to the diver, being admitted by the same type of valve as used with the aqualung.

THE ISLAND OF RHODES AND
ADJACENT ISLANDS

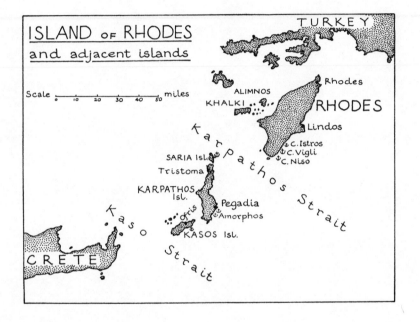

The Eastern Gateway to the Aegean; the passage from N.E. Crete to Rhodes

KASO STRAIT with emergency
 anchorages
ISLAND OF KASOS
 The Port (Ofris)
ISLAND OF KARPATHOS
 Anchorage at Amorphos
 Pegadia
 Tristoma
 The Islet of Saria and Palatea
  anchorage

KARPATHOS STRAIT
ISLAND OF RHODES
Anchorages off the S.E. Coast:
 Cape Nisos
 Cape Vigli
 Cape Istros
 Lindos
 The Harbours of Rhodes
 Mandraki Yacht Harbour
 The Commercial Port

6

The Island of Rhodes and Adjacent Islands

THE EASTERN GATEWAY TO THE AEGEAN

The passage from N.E. Crete to Rhodes

Both the Kaso and Karpathos Straits have a navigable width of about 25 miles; the summer winds blow freshly from the north-westerly quarter.

During the summer, sailing vessels from Crete making for Rhodes are recommended to pass northward of Kasos (but within the protection of the rocky islets off the N.W. coast), thence under the lee of Karpathos—keeping a couple of miles off on account of the strong gusts from the tall mountain range. Thence under the lee of Rhodes to Mandraki Harbour. Sheltered anchorages on this route are given in detail under the heading of each island. Motor yachts

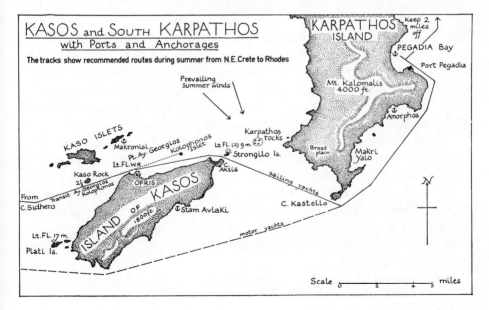

may prefer to pass the S.E. side of Kasos although it is not such an interesting route. Day passages are recommended as the temporary anchorages are unlit.

The **Kaso Strait** is used by local traffic and a few larger vessels plying between Greece and Egyptian ports. It is 25 miles wide, but for $1\frac{1}{2}$ miles off the Cretan shore it is encumbered by rocks. The current is usually south-going but is much influenced by winds.

Approaching the north side of Kasos Island, a yacht should converge on the N.W. coast so as to clear the Kaso Rock ($2\frac{1}{2}$ fathoms) as shown on Chart 2824, i.e. Point St George in transit with Kolophonos Islet. After passing Point Ay. Georgios the steep-to coast may be followed to the N.E. Thence pass between Strongilo Islet and Cape Aktis, head towards the southern tip of Karpathos (Kastello Point).

> **Note.** The Karpathos Rocks (6 feet under water) should be kept in mind. Emergency anchorages:—
>
> (*a*) Under the lee of Kasos Island in an open bay close west of Stam Avlaki.
> (*b*) On the S.E. side of Karpathos, either at Makri Yalo, or in the N.W. corner of Amorphos Bay.

When caught in bad weather north of Kasos caiques use an anchorage under the lee of the rocky islets where there is good shelter in convenient depths on a sandy bottom. The low-lying islet of Makronisi is claimed to be the best choice, though with the advent of the new port of Ofris doubtless some of the caiques would prefer to make use of this instead.

The Island of Kasos mountainous and barren, lying between Karpathos and Crete, has half a dozen hamlets, and since 1962 the small port of **Ofris**. The mail steamer calls twice a week, and after a hazardous manoeuvre can just squeeze into the port. In the event of a strong Meltemi the steamer anchors on the lee of the island about 4 miles S.W. of Strongilo Islet (between Stam Avlaki and Phira Rocks), and communicates by boat with the shore.

The main village of Ofris built round the shores of the bay, accommodates most of the island's 1,200 inhabitants. Little more than a hundred years ago the population was more than five times as large and, though then without its own harbour, Kasos shipping could be seen in many ports of the Mediterranean. Egypt attracted many of the young men, 5,000 of whom left the island and emigrated at the time of the construction of the Suez Canal. It is claimed that the pilot of the leading ship in the procession at the opening of the Canal was a sailor from Kasos.

Kasos now grows enough for its own consumption, but it is a primitive and somewhat unattractive little island. A new hotel, to encourage tourists, has been built.

The Island of Karpathos is long, mountainous and narrow, lacking an adequately sheltered harbour suitable for a yacht in the summer months. There are some indentations, but strong gusts of wind off the mountains sweep down upon the S.E. coast during the Meltemi season. Tristoma, the only well-sheltered harbour in Karpathos lies on the north west coast. It is closed all the summer and autumn months because of the dangerous sea breaking at its mouth. The port-of-call is Pegadia on the south-eastern shores, where a break-water and quay have recently been constructed.

The tall mountain range, rising to nearly 4,000 feet, forms the spine of the island; it runs from end to end and causes hard gusts to sweep down to the S.E. shores, thus limiting the places where landing is possible. In addition to Pegadia there are some small, well-sheltered sandy bays on the S.E. end of the island, where the land is lower and the valleys are more fertile, and there are signs of cultivation. At **Makri Yalo** the adjoining cove, **Amorphos,** is the more suitable for temporary anchorage.

Pegadia, now known as Port Karpathos, the principal village of the island, has recently had some port improvements including the building of a mole with a broad quay.

> **Approach and Anchorage.** Chart 2824 shows the anchorage. The new mole, 100 yards long, runs in a N.W. direction from a small projection on the north side of the town; it does not provide shelter against the mountain gusts which drive a vessel hard against the quay. It is advisable for a yacht to lay out an anchor and to make use of warps to hold her off.
>
> Depths are adequate nearly to the root of the mole, and the bottom is mud. Shelter is poor and there is often a swell. It is sometimes preferable to anchor in the northern corner of the bay, as suggested in *Sailing Directions.*
>
> A yacht should bear in mind that when the steamer calls she takes up most of the space alongside the quay.
>
> **Facilities.** There are a few provision shops, spring water in some of the houses, a restaurant, a new hotel and one or two tavernas. The mail boat calls twice a week.

Only a few hundred people live in the village around the port, but nearly 6,000 on the whole island, and although so close to Rhodes, life here is surprisingly primitive. A large number of the men receive remittances from England, the United States, Italy and elsewhere, where they have worked for most of their lives.

British charts sometimes use the name Scarpanto, the Italian form for Karpathos.

Tristoma on the N.W. coast is an attractive and out-of-the way harbour with half a dozen houses, 3 hours by mule from the nearest village. It cannot be used during the Meltemi season or during strong onshore winds.

> **Approach.** Chart 1666 illustrates the topography of the port. In fresh north winds such an alarming sea is whipped up at the entrance, that the port is closed all the summer months.
> **Note.** The ruined church shown on the chart no longer exists.
> **Anchorage.** This should be chosen according to weather conditions.
> **Facilities.** One can usually buy sufficient bread, flour, or meat for daily needs from the inhabitants who are friendly people quite untouched by foreigners.

A number of small villages can be seen scattered around the mountain slopes, and in Arcassa remnants of Venetian architecture still survive. The inhabitants still wear locally-made coral necklaces and sometimes filigree work. The island produces hardly any exports; the iron and silver mines once exploited by the Romans and later by the Knights of Rhodes have long since ceased working.

One of the few reasons for visiting Karpathos is to see the interesting national dress worn by the women in the north of the island. They may be seen in the fields any day of the week wearing long boots and white breeches with a white skirt, looped up when working.

The little Island of Saria in the north, is separated from the shore of Karpathos by a very narrow, shallow channel. About $1\frac{1}{4}$ miles south of Aimunte Point (its N.E. extremity) is anchorage in the small sandy bay of Palatea; a number of ruins can be seen all round the shores. A few shepherds come here in summer, but it is very seldom that a yacht calls.

The Karpathos Strait, separating Karpathos from Rhodes, is without danger—usually the current sets southward, but is influenced by the direction of the wind. The landfall at Rhodes should be made in daylight as the islets lying eastward of C. Prasonisi are unlit and offshore a current sets towards N.W.

THE ISLAND OF RHODES
The most beautiful is the free island of Rhodes.
PLINY XXXVI

The largest island and capital of the Dodecanese with green mountainous scenery, Rhodes has a long and interesting history.

In addition to the main port of Mandraki and the anchorage at Lindos, *Sailing Directions* refer to a number of places in open bays off the S.E. coast suitable as a lee nearly all the summer months. (Chart 1667.)

Cape Nisos. The coves under this cape are sandy and there is good shelter.

Cape Vigli. A ruined tower is conspicuous standing on the cape. Yachts have found satisfactory anchorage N.E. of the point with the tower bearing 177°, good holding on sand and no swell with moderate N.W. winds. No sign of habitation.

Cape Istros. Let go near a jetty on the S.W. shore where caiques are sometimes to be seen at anchor.

Lindos, one of the three Hellenic cities, lies at the top of a high headland whose sides fall abruptly into the sea. Beneath it is **Port Lindos,** a sheltered summer anchorage from which one may conveniently land to visit the acropolis. (See photograph facing page 108.)

> **Approach.** See plan on Chart 1666, which is not entirely accurate for depths or under-water delineation. There are no harbour lights, so that, except under a bright moon and with previous knowledge, entry by night would be difficult.
>
> **Anchorage.** Let go in about 5 fathoms as near the landing place as you can get. The nature of the bottom varies, being in some places mud or sand on flat rock and occasional ridges of weed which afford poor holding. There is a good shelter except between E. and S.E.
>
> **Facilities.** A path leads up to the village which has a small hotel and restaurant, and a few provision shops. There is daily bus communication with Rhodes.

This place is well worth a visit, and it makes a pleasant day's sail from the town of Rhodes and back during the Meltemi season when there should be a broad reach and smooth water both ways. The acropolis of Lindos, set on a rock high above the sea, is one of the most spectacular sites in Greece. Here is evidence of the whole history of the island, dramatically and lucidly displayed: there is the classical Greek colonnade which caps the high platform of the acropolis with the temple of Athena Lindos, the ruined Byzantine church, and the castle of the Knights. Even the Turks have left a fortification to round off this long tale.

Beneath it is the modern village formerly celebrated for its ceramics; it is pleasant to get away from the tourists and wander among the little white houses, many of which show signs of Venetian influence and contain examples of the once famous Rhodian pottery.

THE HARBOURS OF RHODES

The three harbours flanking the eastern seaboard of the city are shown on the plan taken from Chart 1666. The new Port Akandia has taken the place of the very inadequate Emborikos as a commercial port and its long breakwater is largely the extension of a far earlier mole.

The yacht harbour of Mandraki, originally an ancient port modernized by the Italians, formerly accommodated the caiques; but now that they have been moved out there is more space for the ever-increasing number of yachts.

Mandraki Yacht Harbour.

Approaches. Entering Mandraki Harbour the extensive medieval walls of the old city come into view as well as the modern pseudo-Venetian buildings close to the quayside.

By day there is no difficulty in the approach. By night, however, if coming from southward along the coast, caution is necessary to ensure clearing off-lying shoals.

The light on Fort St Nicholas can be clearly distinguished from afar; but the weaker light marking the extremity of the dangerous rocky point on the north side of the approach has, on a number of occasions, been washed away by winter gales and subsequently replaced. The last time it was washed away was before the loss of the yacht *Trenchemer* (Robert Somerset) in a S.E. gale during darkness on the night of 27th February, 1965. The light was eventually set up on a safer site a few yards further inshore and was still in position in 1970. Its present characteristics: Qk. Fl.(G). shows over the arc of the approach and red through an arc towards west. Characteristics of the other lights can be found in *The Light List*.

In strong E. to S.E. winds a yacht is strongly advised against trying to enter Mandraki; she should make for Trianda Bay instead.

Berth. Yachts usually berth beyond the second 'T'-shaped jetty on the western shore, with stern to the quay. The bottom is mud and the water rather foul. Although the harbour is completely enclosed, during winter gales from the S.E., heavy seas sometimes come over the breakwater.

Recently the harbour has been dredged and the southern quay much improved.

A number of caiques from the Aegean use the port, always berthing off the breakwater.

Officials. Health, Customs, Immigration and Harbour-Master (office on the harbour front), this being a Port of Entry.

Facilities. Water is laid on by a hydrant near the root of the jetty; its supply and hose can be arranged by the Harbour Master. There is petrol and diesel fuel available from a pump at the quay.

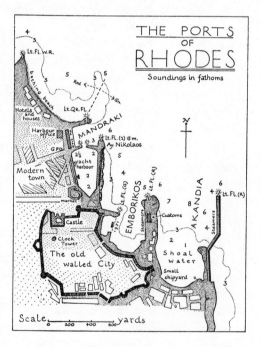

THE PORTS OF RHODES
Soundings in fathoms

118

Plenty of good shops are close at hand, also the white octagonal market. There are many large modern hotels, and several restaurants of various standards. The Bank of Athens and Ionian Bank have large branches here. A casino has been opened.

Repairs both by mechanics and skilled artisans are hard to come by, except in the Old City; and the two shipyards, accustomed to ordinary caique slipping and repair work, have but little experience of yacht work.

A special Customs Agreement between the Dodecanese and the Greek Government enables certain supplies such as English spirits and tinned provisions to be bought cheaply; other articles are reasonably priced including tinned meat from Holland and Denmark, biscuits and cosmetics from England. The best wine comes from C.A.I.R.; excellent draught red and white: bottled 'Rodos', 'Moulin Rouge' and 'Chevalier' can also be bought.

The fast steamers from Piraeus run five times a week (about 20 hours) and berth at the South Harbour. There is a daily air service with Athens; also air communication with Crete twice a week.

The Commercial Port has recently been enlarged, and the new port of Akandia, completed in 1971, will have 500 yards of quays.

The town of today was much restored and newly built during the 30-year Italian domination between the two World Wars, and for many years it has been a large flourishing summer resort with more than a hundred hotels and a port of call for many cruise ships. The medieval architecture of the Knights of St John is to be seen everywhere in the old city, which is well worth visiting.

On leaving the town, the sight of the country with its pleasant villages soon restores the feeling of being in Greece. There are the other two Hellenic cities of Kamiros and Halysus, and castles of the Knights of St John on the north-west coast.

From here can be seen the two unimportant small islands lying close off the north-west coast of Rhodes—Alimnos and Khalki, described in *The Aegean*. Both have sheltered bays but are rather deep for anchoring.

These are only some of the places not to be missed, and which can be reached by bus or taxi.

Earlier history of Rhodes tells of the tremendous sieges, first in the third century B.C. and again in the sixteenth century A.D. from both of which there is evidence today. Following the earlier sieges Rhodes became one of the most prosperous centres of the Hellenistic world, and its city was nearly five times the size of the Old City of today. Its acropolis built on Mount Smith (named after Admiral Sir Sidney Smith of Napoleonic times) has been excavated and the foundations of a stadium, theatre and two temples unearthed. But the medieval architecture, standing nearly intact, is that set up by the Knights during their two centuries of ruling the island from 1309 to 1522. It was during this period that the strategic position of Rhodes was used to full advantage. Building a strong navy, the Knights were continually destroying Arab shipping, successfully fighting the fleets of Islam and making descents upon their Syrian and African strongholds.

The famous Colossus, a wonder of the world, probably stood where Fort St Nicholas now is, and rose to a height of slightly more than 100 feet. It was a statue to Helion, the sun god, standing erect and not as the post-cards show, astride the harbour. The skin of the statue was formed of bronze made from the captured siege engines of the Syrian king, Peliorcetes; it was probably fastened by dowels to an inner core of iron and limestone blocks. It stood for only half a century having been toppled into the sea by a destructive earthquake in 227 B.C. The broken metal lay in the shallow water of the harbour for 900 years, when it was bought for scrap by a Levantine Jew who took it back to Tyre in Syria where the metal was first moulded.

Although Rhodes is now the most popular tourist resort in Greece, it should not be forgotten that this island owes its prominent part in early history to its strategic position at the gateway to the Aegean: from Hellenistic days to early Roman times maritime supremacy gave Rhodes prosperity and culture. In medieval times Rhodes together with Famagusta were considered to be the 'two strongest holds in the empire of the great Turke'. Its strategic position was rather belatedly recognized by the British in the Second World War when, in the autumn of 1943, their foothold in the Aegean islands had to be abandoned. This disaster cost the British and Greek navies six destroyers, two submarines, and a number of light craft, the air forces more than 100 aircraft, the army nearly 5,000 men. Only too late was it realized that Rhodes should have first been captured from the Germans before attempting to seize the Aegean islands.

> *Roll on, thou deep and dark blue Ocean—roll!*
> *Ten thousand fleets sweep over thee in vain;*
> *Man marks the earth with ruin—his control*
> *Stops with the shore;*
> BYRON *Childe Harold*

Index